DATA FUSION

METHODS, APPLICATIONS AND RESEARCH

RESEARCH METHODOLOGY AND DATA ANALYSIS

Additional books in this series can be found on Nova's website under the Series tab.

Additional e-books in this series can be found on Nova's website under the eBooks tab.

RESEARCH METHODOLOGY AND DATA ANALYSIS

DATA FUSION

METHODS, APPLICATIONS AND RESEARCH

VERES ALBERT
AND
ERÔSS ABA
EDITORS

nova
science publishers
New York

NOTICE TO THE READER

Library of Congress Cataloging-in-Publication Data

ISBN: 978-1-53612-720-1

Published by Nova Science Publishers, Inc. † New York

CONTENTS

PREFACE

In the first chapter, Sergey A. Sakulin, PhD and Alexander N. Alfimtsev, PhD discuss fuzzy integral, a powerful metaoperator, and its applications. In the second chapter, Bruno G. Botelho and Adriana S. Franca discuss the concept of data fusion and how it might be applied in different areas of food analysis to improve the information range regarding samples. In the third and final chapter, Carlo Quaranta and Giorgio Balzarotti compare a new data fusion equation with an approach that has been familiarized in previous literature.

Chapter 1 - The data fusion technology allows one to combine heterogeneous information coming from different sources in digital application areas. Criteria aggregation operators are one of the effective ways to implement data fusion. But selecting the appropriate aggregation operator for a specific application is a great challenge. Nevertheless, there are metaoperators that generalize simple operators and allow to select the type and properties of the resulting operator using direct parameters control. One of the powerful metaoperators is the fuzzy integral. Fuzzy integral with respect to fuzzy measure allows taking into account the phenomenon of dependence between criteria. Due to this it is possible to reflect the expert knowledge more accurately without making the model simplification which is the assumption of the aggregation criteria independence. The problems of fuzzy integral applications and effective methods of overcoming them are discussed in this chapter. Also the central trends in practical applications for this relatively new apparatus are reviewed. In the application of Web personalization will be discussed in detail the ability to use fuzzy integrals without expert sets of fuzzy measure and covering all stages of the personalization from a user's query to fusion of an individual user's profiles in a single parameter of users group. An application of fuzzy integral in the method of expert knowledge formalization about the usability of web pages is analyzed. As well as the problem of fuzzy measures identification for aggregating user criteria is studied. Examples of assessments for main usability criteria and results of leading web pages evaluation are provided. An application of determining the weights in information retrieval using the fuzzy integral is given. Information retrieval based on weighted zone scoring creates the assignment weight for each zone or each field in the document data. All these weights are usually obtained by machine learning methods with weights determination based on fuzzy integral that allows to calculate the more objective relevance and reach higher scoring accuracy.

Chapter 2 - In recent years, the application of chemometric methods in food analysis has gained great importance. It allows for fast, simple and, most of the time, non-destructive determination of micro and macro constituents, physical and chemical properties, and detection of adulteration, among other possibilities. Foodstuffs are known for being highly complex matrices, and one single analytical technique may, sometimes, not provide all the necessary information for the required method. A natural step for the development of methods for this type of matrix is to combine two or more techniques, in order to increase the range of information about the samples and exploit the possibility of merging information from different sources. This data fusion can lead to a more accurate knowledge about the samples and also provide methods with improved prediction capacity. In this review, the concept of data fusion, its fundaments and its application in different areas of food analysis will be explored.

Chapter 3 - The problem for a data fusion system of a non-exhaustive number of common measurements from sensors of different types is faced here. In the presence of a suite of heterogeneous sensors, the data fusion process has to deal with the management of different information that is generally not directly comparable. Hence, the process of association and fusion between the data of tracks from different sensors is complicated by the fact of having a limited number of comparable measurements: also, objects located at a great distance from each other can give rise to wrong associations between them. The analysis is carried out considering the fusion of data between radar and Infrared Search and Track (IRST) where the measurement of the range is achieved by radar only and demonstrates the need for a tracking process of the fused tracks that allows the effective use of algorithms such as, for example, the Joint Probabilistic Data Association (JPDA) in order to reduce the probability of bad associations between tracks from different sensors. Moreover, because of the tracking process of the fused tracks, it is suggested to use a new fusion equation that exploits the characteristics of the sensors in use that performs better in the presence of fast variation of the state of the tracks from the different sensors. Simulation results demonstrate the effectiveness of the algorithms, specifically the fusion process, tracking and correctness of association among tracks from different sensors. A comparison between the new fusion equation and a known approach from the literature is also performed.

In: Data Fusion
Editors: V. Albert and E. Aba

ISBN: 978-1-53612-720-1
© 2017 Nova Science Publishers, Inc.

Chapter 1

DATA FUSION BASED ON THE FUZZY INTEGRAL: MODEL, METHODS AND APPLICATIONS

Sergey A. Sakulin, PhD
and Alexander N. Alfimtsev, PhD

Department of Information Systems and Telecommunications
Bauman Moscow State Technical University,
Moscow, Russia

ABSTRACT

The data fusion technology allows one to combine heterogeneous information coming from different sources in digital application areas. Criteria aggregation operators are one of the effective ways to implement data fusion. But selecting the appropriate aggregation operator for a specific application is a great challenge. Nevertheless, there are metaoperators that generalize simple operators and allow to select the type and properties of the resulting operator using direct parameters control. One of the powerful metaoperators is the fuzzy integral. Fuzzy integral with respect to fuzzy measure allows taking into account the phenomenon of dependence between criteria. Due to this it is possible to reflect the expert knowledge more accurately without making the model simplification which is the assumption of the aggregation criteria independence.

The problems of fuzzy integral applications and effective methods of overcoming them are discussed in this chapter. Also the central trends in practical applications for this relatively new apparatus are reviewed. In the application of Web personalization will be discussed in detail the ability to use fuzzy integrals without expert sets of fuzzy measure and covering all stages of the personalization from a user's query to fusion of an individual user's profiles in a single parameter of users group. An application of fuzzy integral in the method of expert knowledge formalization about the usability of web pages is analyzed. As well as the problem of fuzzy measures identification for aggregating user criteria is studied. Examples of assessments for main usability criteria and results of leading web pages evaluation are provided. An application of determining the weights in information retrieval using the fuzzy integral is given. Information retrieval based on weighted zone scoring creates the assignment weight for each zone or each field in the document data. All these weights are usually obtained by machine learning methods with weights determination based on fuzzy integral that allows to calculate the more objective relevance and reach higher scoring accuracy.

Keywords: Information technology, machine learning, ensemble methods, regularization strategy, soft computing, fuzzy logic, aggregation operators, expert knowledge, human-computer interaction, user interface, usability testing, interactive information retrieval

1. INTRODUCTION

The technology of data fusion allows one to combine information coming from different sources in many application areas. Criteria aggregation operators are one of the ways to implement this technology. The task of selecting the appropriate aggregation operator for a specific application is not trivial [1, 2]. Nevertheless, there are aggregation operators that generalize some other operators and allow to select the type and properties of the resulting operator by changing their parameters. One of the generalizing operators is the fuzzy integral [3].

Fuzzy measures and integrals were proposed in the monograph "Theory of capacities" [4] published by Gustave Choquet in 1953 which happened earlier than publication of well-known paper [5] by Lotfi Zadeh, the founder of the theory of fuzzy sets took place. In this paper Choquet proposed the use of non-additive measures which he called the capacities. Although there is no direct connection between the theory of fuzzy measures and fuzzy sets theory, they are well combined in sense that the fuzzy integral is a convenient tool to aggregate the values of membership functions of fuzzy sets. Later Choquet's ideas were developed by Sugeno in his unpublished thesis [6] referred in many later works. Sugeno proposed two types of aggregation operators based on Choquet measures. One of these types is called fuzzy discrete Choquet integral and the second is called fuzzy discrete Sugeno integral. As it is said later in this chapter, the words "fuzzy" and "discrete" are often omitted for brevity. Sugeno integral is used to aggregation for which the result depends on criteria values order on the real axis (ordinal scale aggregation) [7]. Result of aggregation using Choquet integral depends on the value of each criterion [7, 8]. Thus, the Choquet integral is better suited for quantitative criteria aggregation while the Sugeno integral is more convenient for qualitative aggregation [9].

Fuzzy integral allows taking into account the phenomenon of dependence between criteria. Due to this it is possible to reflect the expert knowledge more accurately without making the model simplification which is the assumption of independence of the aggregation criteria. The model of fuzzy integral and its implementation methods are considered in this chapter. Following practical applications for this relatively new apparatus are reviewed in detail: the method for Web personalization based on fuzzy integral and recognition of user activity [10]; the method of expert knowledge formalization about the usability of web pages [11]; the method of determining the weights in Information retrieval using the fuzzy Choquet integral [12].

2. AGGREGATION, FUZZY MEASURES
AND THE FUZZY INTEGRAL

According to [7-9] numeric criteria aggregation is a method combining them into a single numeric criterion (aggregation result) for the expression of the cumulative effects of these criteria. Aggregation is used in data fusion, pattern recognition, and multi-criteria decision-making problems. Aggregation operator is often called a function of variables (criteria) having some desired properties, each of variables being defined in the interval [0,1]. The domain of this function is also the interval [0,1].

The choice of the operator caused by the information about criteria aggregation which can be obtained from an expert [1]. The simplest and most widely used criteria aggregation operator is traditionally weighted arithmetic mean operator. This operator, however, does not allow one to formalize expert knowledge about dependencies between criteria [13]. If the aggregated criteria are interdependent then fuzzy integral with respect to fuzzy measure can be used instead of the weighted arithmetic mean operator for formalizing that dependence. Choquet integral with respect to fuzzy measure is a generalization of the weighted arithmetic mean operator in case of dependence between criteria of aggregation.

Fuzzy measure expresses the subjective weight or importance of each subset of criteria and defined as follows [7].

Fuzzy (discrete) measure is a function $\psi:\ 2^J \to [0,1]$, where 2^J is the set of all subsets of the criteria index set $J = \{1, ..., H\}$, which satisfies the following conditions:

1) $\psi(\varnothing) = 0$, $\psi(J) = 1$;

2) $\forall D, B \subseteq J:\ D \subseteq B \Rightarrow \psi(D) \leq \psi(B)$

Further, we will omit the curly brackets writing i, ij instead of $\{i\}$, $\{i, j\}$ respectively. Instead of the "criterion of the index $i \in J$ " we will also use the "criterion i" instead of the "criteria index set J" we will use the "set of criteria J" both done for brevity reason.

Firstly, we consider the basic concepts used in the fuzzy measures theory. Shapley [14] proposed a definition of the criterion importance coefficient based on several natural axioms. In the context of the fuzzy measures theory Shapley index for the criterion $i \in J$ with respect to fuzzy measure ψ is determined by the following expression [15]:

$$\Phi_{Sh}(i) := \sum_{D \subseteq (J-i)} \frac{(|J|-|D|-1)!|D|!}{|J|!}\left[\psi(D \cup i) - \psi(D)\right] \tag{1}$$

Murofushi and Soneda proposed an interaction index between criteria [16]. This index is used to express the sign and degree of interaction between criteria and is determined by the following expression:

$$I(i,j) := \sum_{D \subseteq (J-\{i,j\})} \frac{(|J|-|D|-2)!|D|!}{(|J|-1)!}\left[\psi(D \cup ij) - \psi(D \cup i) - \psi(D \cup j) + \psi(D)\right] \tag{2}$$

Marichall [17] identified the main types of dependencies between criteria in the context of aggregation with fuzzy integral.

Correlation is the best known of the dependencies between criteria. Two criteria $i, j \in J$ are positively (negatively) correlated if expert can observe a positive (negative) correlation between the contributions of two criteria to the aggregation result.

Substitutiveness (complementarity) is another type of dependence. The idea of formalizing this type of dependencies using fuzzy measures was proposed by Murofushi and Soneda [16]. Considering again two criteria $i, j \in J$ we can suppose that the expert believes that satisfying only one criterion causes almost the same effect as satisfying of both. Here the importance of a pair of criteria is close to the importance of each of them individually, even if other criteria are present. In this case we see that criteria i and j almost substitutive or interchangeable.

Interaction index (2) is positive as soon as criteria $i, j \in J$ are negatively correlated or complementary. On the other hand, it is negative when criteria $i, j \in J$ are positive correlated or substitutive.

Preferred dependence (preferred independence) is the type of dependency which is well known in the multiattribute utility theory [18, 19]. We suppose that expert's preferences on the set of criteria realizations A are known and expressed as the partial weak order over A. The set A is usually consists of parameters available for assessment objects. Denote $\mathbf{g}_D$ the realization of criteria g_i where $i \in D$, denote $\mathbf{g}_{J-D}$ the realization of criteria g_i where $i \in J - D$. The subset $D \subset J$ of criteria is said to be preferentially independent of $J - D$ if for all pair $\mathbf{g}_D$, $\mathbf{g}'_D$ we have from $(\mathbf{g}_D, \mathbf{g}_{J-D}) \succeq (\mathbf{g}'_D, \mathbf{g}_{J-D})$ for some realization $\mathbf{g}_{J-D}$ follows $(\mathbf{g}_D, \mathbf{g}_{J-D}) \succeq (\mathbf{g}'_D, \mathbf{g}_{J-D})$ for all realizations $\mathbf{g}_{J-D}$. Otherwise subset $D \subset J$ preferably depends on the subset $J - D$. The full set of criteria J mutually preferably independent if subset D preferably independent of subset $J - D$ for each subset D. It is known [7, 18, 19] that if certain criteria are preferably dependent on others then the additive aggregation operators can not reflect the expert's preferences. In particular, in this case it is impossible to use the weighted arithmetic mean operator.

The Choquet integral of the criteria $g_1, ..., g_H$ with respect to ψ is defined by $C_\psi(g_1, ..., g_H) := \sum_{h=1}^{H} g_{(h)} [\psi(A_{(h)}) - \psi(A_{(h+1)})]$, where (*) indicates a permutation of J such that $g_{(1)} \leq g_{(H)}$. Also $A_{(h)} = \{(h), ..., (H)\}$ and $A_{(H+1)} = \varnothing$. Choquet integral using for dependent criteria aggregation is considered in [3]. Particularly criteria preferred dependence modeled by Choquet integral is discussed in [17].

The Sugeno integral of the criteria $g_1, ..., g_H$ with respect to ψ is defined by $S_\psi(g_1, ..., g_H) := \max_{h=1}^{h=H} \left[\min(g_h, \psi(A_{(h)})) \right]$ where (*) indicates a permutation of J such that $g_{(h)} \geq g_{(h+1)}$ for $h \geq 1$. Also $A_{(h)} = \{g_{(1)}, ..., g_{(h)}\}$ for $h \geq 1$ and $A_{(0)} = \varnothing$. Sugeno integral using for dependent criteria aggregation is considered in [3]. Particularly criteria preferred dependence modeled by Sugeno integral is discussed in [9].

According to Grabisch [20] "From the beginning of the application of fuzzy measures and integrals to multicriteria evaluating problems, it has always been felt that the non-additivity of fuzzy measure was able to model dependency between criteria, but until recently, this point was not investigated in a rigorous manner, for nobody defined precisely what he intends by "dependent." If a fuzzy measure is additive, the criteria do not interact with each other and the interaction indices of these criteria are equal to zero. Therefore, if the expert thinks the criteria mutually preferably independent, the corresponding interaction indices are equal to zero. If the expert suggests that the criteria are preferably dependent then it is possible to formalize this only by means of partial weak order on the set of criteria realizations (training set). No other method of formalization of the criteria preferred dependence and independence has not been proposed.

To use the fuzzy integral preliminary we have to identify the fuzzy measure on the basis of expert knowledge. This identification is complicated by exponential increasing complexity in the sense that it is necessary to set a value of fuzzy measure for each subset of criteria. Setting the values of all 2^H coefficients of the fuzzy measure $\psi(D)$, $D \subseteq J$ is very difficult or even impossible for the expert. Note that even in case of three criteria for determining the fuzzy measure it is necessary to obtain $2^3 = 8$ coefficients. Despite this complexity fuzzy integral still can be applied in practice. For this Grabisch proposed the concept of κ- order fuzzy measure or κ- additive fuzzy measure [21]. This order κ can be less than the number of aggregated criteria, $\kappa < |J| = H$. Essence of the κ- additivity concept consists in simplification of the task of fuzzy measures determining by excluding from consideration the dependencies between more than κ criteria. According to the κ- additivity concept in most practical cases it is possible to use the

Choquet integral with respect to 2-order fuzzy measure or, equivalently, the 2-order Choquet integral because it allows to model the interaction between the criteria while remaining relatively simple [21]. The paper [22] is entirely devoted to the question under what conditions such a simplification (using of the 2-order Choquet integral) is correct. This work presents necessary conditions that should satisfy the expert preferences in order that they can be formalized using the 2-order Choquet integral.

In addition to increasing complexity there also appears a problem of the expert's understanding of fuzzy measure coefficients meaning [20]. To solve this problem Grabisch [23] proposed the idea of the graphical interpretation of the 2-order Choquet integral. This interpretation is represented by a constraint line of values of the interaction index and Shapley indexes for two criteria on the coordinate plane. This idea has been applied to identify the fuzzy measure using a hierarchical diagram of pairwise comparisons ("diamond pairwise comparisons method") [24, 25]. This approach to fuzzy measure identification has two main difficulties. First, because the expert considers each pair of criteria separately he (she) does not have a complete picture of aggregation and can formulate his (her) preferences so that the fuzzy measure identification problem based on these preferences obviously will not have the solution. Second, the "diamond" form of scale is not trivial for the expert. These difficulties can be overcome by an apparent indication of the restrictions imposed on expert preferences [22] and also by careful tutoring of the expert of a graphic interpretation method.

Visualization of 2-order Choquet integral offered in [26] can be both alternative and addition of graphic interpretation (Figure 1). This visualization is based on one-to-one comparison between mathematical object (2-order Choquet integral) and physical object (the lever fixed in the center by a spring with a simple stiffness factor which can rotate round a horizontal axis).

The idea of the balance model [8] is to establish a strong relationship of the physical model and a mathematical aggregation operator. The balance model must reflect the influence of the interaction indices of criteria on result of aggregation. A range of values of these indices is an interval $[-1,1]$ [16]. Taking into consideration this range of values, we have chosen the same interval for scale of the lever. We have chosen 0 as a neutral element on the scale of the lever (or places of its strengthening).

The physical model appropriate to this modification is represented on a Figure 1, where $I(1,2)$ is the weight corresponding to interaction index between criteria, g_1, g_2 are the distances of the weights to the fulcrum corresponding to values of criteria, $\psi(1)$, $\psi(2)$ are the weights corresponding to appropriate fuzzy measures, x is the angle between the lever and the horizon corresponding to result of aggregation. Without any restriction, we can suppose that x is very small (close to zero). The balance equation of this model can be expressed with using of Newton's Second Law by projecting on the horizontal axis and for x close to zero:

$$kx = g_1\psi(1) + g_2\psi(2) + I(1,2)\min(g_1, g_2)$$

where k is the constant of stiffness of the spring.

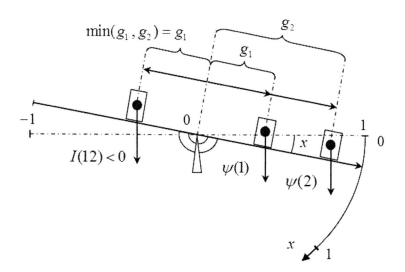

Figure 1. Visualization of 2-order Choquet integral.

If $I(i,j) < 0$ then weight corresponding to interaction index should be placed on distance $\min(g_i, g_j)$ to the left from the fulcrum. If $I(i,j) > 0$ then weight corresponding to interaction index should be placed on distance $\min(g_i, g_j)$ to the right from the fulcrum. We can easily generalize this result to H criteria for $k = 1$:

$$x = \sum_{i=1}^{H} g_i \psi(i) + \sum_{\{i,j\} \subseteq J} I(i,j) \min(g_i, g_j)$$

This expression is equivalent of the Choquet integral with respect to 2-order fuzzy measure ψ.

In the manner described, loads with weights corresponding to interaction indices $I(ij)$ (2) and fuzzy measures $\psi(i)$ are established on the lever. This approach relies on the natural intuition peculiar to many people in regard to the well-known physical object and allows the expert to have a clear intuitive understanding of behavior of 2-order Choquet integral. This visualization reveals the expert preferences in the form of limitations on the fuzzy measure. Fuzzy measure can be identified based on these limitations and implemented in order to build a lever. This process is iterative and continues until 2-order Choquet integral with respect to identified fuzzy measure will satisfy the expert. This approach is also facing difficulties. First, when the number of criteria (from about four to five with additional loads that are associated with interaction indices) the expert is having difficulty accepting this visualization (as we know from psychology the average person is able to simultaneously keep in attention no more than 7 items). Second, such visualization considers fuzzy measure of each separate criterion and Shapley indices (1) are visualized for each criterion separately. The above puts extra pressure on the experts' attention. It seems that both of these difficulties can be overcome by careful design of procedures for working with the expert taking into account specifics of each subject domain.

In the process of expert knowledge formalization using different approaches we need to select a mathematical method for the fuzzy measure identification. These methods differ in the types of information that is required as input. A review of methods for fuzzy measure identification in relation to the utility theory is presented in [27].

Method based on least squares is not well suited for solving practical problems because it requires desired values of aggregation result as input. But the experts are not always able to set such values [27].

Method based on the maximum split is well suited to meet the challenges of recognition, as it maximizes the minimum difference between the results of the aggregation of the training set. The expert describes an sample of each class and ranks them by non-strict order that serves as input to the identification method [28].

Method based on minimization of fuzzy measure variance [29] or maximization of fuzzy measure entropy [30] is the most suited for solving many practical problems. This method is based on the principle of maximum entropy proposed by Jaynes [31]. In relation to the construction of aggregation operators that principle involves the use of all available information about the aggregation criteria but the most unbiased attitude to the inaccessible information. Kojadinovic [29] extended the principle of maximum entropy on the utility theory and developed fuzzy measures identification method based on this. The objective function of this method [29] is defined as the variance of fuzzy measure:

$$F_{MV}(\psi) := \frac{1}{|J|} \sum_{i \in J} \sum_{G \subseteq J-i} \frac{(|J|-|G|-1)!|G|!}{|J|!} \left(\sum_{D \subseteq G} a(D \cup i) - \frac{1}{|J|} \right)^2$$

Corresponding optimization problem takes the following form. Minimize $F_{MV}(\psi)$ under the following constraints:

$$\left\{ \begin{array}{c} \sum_{\substack{D \subseteq G \\ |D| \leq \kappa - 1}} a(D \cup i) \geq 0, \ \forall i \in J, \ \forall G \subseteq J - i \\ \sum_{\substack{D \subseteq G \\ 0 \leq |D| \leq \kappa}} a(D) = 1 \\ C_\psi(\mathbf{g}) - C_\psi(\mathbf{g}') \geq \delta_C \\ \dots \end{array} \right.$$

Here $G \subseteq J$; κ is the order of fuzzy measure ψ; δ_{CH} - indifference threshold that is set by an expert to compare the two results of aggregation; $a(D)$ is set function of a set J, this is called the Möbius function and is defined by the following expression and is given by

$$a(D) = \sum_{G \subseteq D} (-1)^{|D| - |G|} \psi(D) .$$

Fuzzy measure identification by one or another method requires setting indifference threshold values for interaction index and Shapley index and the aggregation result. Usually, this question receives little attention, and it is considered that the expert must specify these values on the grounds of the necessary accuracy [27]. But in practice, the indifference threshold values can be set in such a way that it will cause absence of the fuzzy measure which in its turn is the solution of the identification problem. Way to prevent such situations proposed in [26].

3. REVIEW OF PRACTICAL APPLICATIONS

In the last decade, the number of publications devoted to the application of fuzzy integrals for data fusion has increased significantly. The following practical examples briefly describe the application of fuzzy integral including interface properties evaluation, technical diagnostics, navigation, image processing and improvement, image encryption, forensic anthropology, etc.

In [32] a solution to the problem of determining the degree of software interface usability with the help of this aggregation operator was proposed. This assumes direct expert determination of fuzzy measures by filling in special tables for multiple criteria (about four). For the expert, this method is very difficult task in the case of even a minor increase in the number of criteria. However, this example shows that the use of Choquet integral can improve the accuracy of interface usability evaluation.

Another practical example of the Choquet integral and fuzzy measure application is the analysis of the technological processes state based on fuzzy expert knowledge [26]. The first level of state analysis evaluates the membership functions values of the process parameters. These fuzzy sets are based on the expert knowledge of the process faults. At the second level membership values of the current process state to a particular class of fuzzy states by aggregating membership functions values using Choquet integral and the fuzzy measures is obtained (for example, a class of equipment proper functioning states). Fuzzy measure identification is realized by the maximization fuzzy measure entropy method using visualization. This example confirms the possibility of increasing the accuracy of classification technological processes state to the class of equipment proper functioning states or classes corresponding to the process faults.

Yet another example of application of this mathematical tool is illustrated in the paper [33] which describes the navigation system for pedestrians. The inputs to the system are the subjective assessment of various characteristics of the routes in particular: distance, quality of the road surface, neighborhood picturesque, degree of noise etc. All of these criteria are often linked in a nontrivial way. Therefore, the aggregation of such criteria is conveniently carried out by using the Choquet integral. As a method for the fuzzy measure identification there the least squares method is applied. Despite relatively high complexity of implementation, this example shows the flexibility of the Choquet integral as an aggregation operator of such subjective criteria.

Choquet integral with respect to fuzzy measure is also used in the field of digital image processing (DIP). The paper [34] describes recognition of areas of interest on 3D-tomographic images of electrotechnical parts made of composite materials. As fuzzy measure identification method the relative entropy method is used. Relative entropy method is the development of a variance minimizing method. It adapted for the purposes of recognition and allows getting better results. Four attributes derived from tomographic images are aggregated. The experimental results confirm perceptivity of use related apparatus in the image recognition. In [35] the application of Choquet integral and interval type-2 Choquet integral for the edge detection in digital images is considered. This approach uses morphological gradient technique to obtain criteria for aggregation with help of Choquet integral and fuzzy density intervals for taking uncertainty into account. According to the author: "The Choquet integral is an aggregation operator, which offers a more flexible and realistic approach to model uncertainty." Experimental results showed that the use of this aggregation operator allows to improve the performance of the morphological gradient edge detector.

Another area of Choquet integral DIP application is digital images enhancement. Authors of the paper [36] proposed a method for digital image improving based on the use of the Choquet integral. The experimental results showed that this method can process images with high accuracy comparable to the popular filtration methods, besides the greatest accuracy of processing was obtained using the fuzzy measure identification method based on the maximization fuzzy measure entropy. The authors of the paper [37] proposed an algorithm for image encryption using the fuzzy Choquet integral and the hyper-chaotic Lorentz system. The algorithm is based on a pseudo-random number generator that includes the Choquet integral. Experiments have confirmed that such a scheme allows one to obtain a good encryption result.

Data fusion based on fuzzy integral is also used in the field of the forensic anthropology. In [38] authors applied the fuzzy Sugeno integral to estimate the age-at-death of an individual skeleton. They used the Sugeno integral as the aggregation operator, because in their opinion, this integral is easier to conceptualize than the Choquet integral in the given subject domain. It is shown that the method for estimating the age-at-death based on the use of the fuzzy Sugeno integral has several advantages over single age-at-death estimation methods.

In addition, there are many recent successful applications of data fusion by fuzzy integrals in other areas such as brain-computer interface system based on electroencephalography signal processing [39], multi-criteria supplier selection in automobile industry [40], selection and classification of most significant and pertinent attributes for early breast cancer diagnosis from MRIs [41], multi-criteria evaluation system for animal welfare on farms [42], evaluation of the emergency logistics support capability using discrete Choquet integral [43].

Let's review in detail the above-mentioned applications of data fusion with a fuzzy integral.

3.1. The Method for Web Personalization Based on Fuzzy Aggregation and Recognition of User Activity

This subsection addresses Web personalization based on the analysis of individual user activity. However, human behavior is characterized by uncertainties that should be considered in the personalization algorithms. Fuzzy logic allows taking into account different types of uncertainty. Therefore, the subsection presents a method for Web personalization based on fuzzy integral and recognition of user activity based on aggregation of membership functions' values of user's criteria.

3.1.1. Web Personalization: A Review

The story of the Web began with an essay written by Vannevar Bush, "As We May Think" published in July, 1945 in the Atlantic Monthly [44]. In this essay, Bush described the theory of Memex a proto-hypertext system that was later developed into the World Wide Web.

Today the Web is increasing exponentially and now this phenomenon is more than just a hypertext. The Web began to acquire elements of intelligence. One such element is the ability to adapt to a particular user. For example, the Google search engine allows one to personalize the search based on user search history [45]. Online marketing and advertising are also becoming more individualized, aimed separately at each user (consumer) [46, 47]. Flexible security personalization approaches will allow an Internet or Web service provider to negotiate with its clientele to an agreed-upon personalized security policy [48]. Interface designers suggest using the personality concept, which helps build a personal user's model based on the interests of individuals [49, 50].

Authors of the paper [51] provides the wide research overview in the field of Web personalization. According to [51], Web Personalization is defined as the process of customizing the content and structure of a web site to the specific and individual needs of each user taking advantage of the user's navigation habits. In a more recent review [52], personalization is understood as the process of individualized matching to consumer preferences through automated processes in the Web environment. This review focuses on the marketing aspects of Web personalization and such areas as healthcare, information retrieval, games, education were not considered. In particular, as a possible direction of research, it is proposed to unite the efforts of marketing researchers and computer science researchers: marketing researchers develop consumers' behavior models based on real facts, and computer scientists promote their personalization algorithms based on these models. In addition, the authors in this review point to the contextual factors of web personalization such as cultural effects, timing, personal dispositions and even emotions. The influence of these factors should also be taken into account when building the sustainable Web personalization model.

Today, the main methods for Web personalization are data mining techniques which use clustering algorithms. Clustering is widely used in fields such as machine learning, information retrieval, etc. According to [53] the problem of identifying groups of users naturally lends itself to the use of clustering methods. Data clustering can also be used to generate user profiles based on information about the activity of each user and then for the formation of groups of users based on their profiles. But current clustering methods do not take into account all the factors for successful application in many real tasks. Instead, extensive experimentation with the pattern recognition methods is combined with intensive automatic machine learning which yields both approach and knowledge for resolving a lot of sophisticated problems.

Adapting to a particular user is a difficult task because it is necessary to take into account inherent human uncertainty since man is unstable and spontaneous by nature. Many uncertainties of different kinds are present in the global network, for example, Web pages appear and disappear, the context of search keywords is constantly changing. Therefore, a search on the network is indistinct by its nature. In order to work with this uncertainty using computers it should be formalized in some way. Fuzzy logic allows us to take into account different kinds of uncertainties. Fuzzy clustering of the users' profiles can be used to construct fuzzy rules and conclusions in order to modify queries. The results can be used for knowledge extraction from users' profiles for marketing purposes [54, 55].

However, the simple application of fuzzy logic to personalize the web may not lead to desired results, because it simplifies the actual picture of the user's preference. One of these simplifications is the usage of the weighted arithmetic mean operator for the aggregation of several criteria when each criterion is assigned a weight yet interaction between the criteria is not taken into account [17]. The use of the Sugeno and Choquet fuzzy integrals with respect to fuzzy measure allows us to consider such interactions within the model [56]. But in this case there is a problem of identification of fuzzy measures. This problem is caused not only by exponentially increasing complexity of fuzzy measures based on the criteria number, but by lack of clear understanding of the essence of fuzzy measure concept as well [20]. Usually this problem is solved by means of significant simplification of the model and applying various support tools aimed for the identification of fuzzy measures [24, 25] or by identifying fuzzy measures without expert's presence. For example, the Sugeno fuzzy integral is used to aggregate the search results received from the various search engines on the Web [56].

In this subsection, an approach to personalization in the network using a recognition method based on aggregation of data sources involving the Sugeno and the Choquet fuzzy integrals is suggested. The difference between this approach and existing ones lies in the ability to use the Choquet integral without the necessary expert set of fuzzy measures (which is almost impossible in real systems), to cover all stages of the personalization starting from aggregation of single user's query parameters and ending with aggregating of individual user's profiles to a single parameter of a group of users. First, we address the necessary concepts and definitions of fuzzy integrals. Second, we turn to the procedure of forming the users' profiles (a user's profile is an information set which involves queries, email, habits, etc.). The subsection concludes with an explanation of user profile recognition method and experimental results.

3.1.2. Fuzzy Measure and Integral in Web Personalization Tasks

In this subsection the criteria for data fusion are the values of the fuzzy set membership functions and the concept of g_λ-fuzzy measures is used. Therefore in this subsection we change the notation introduced in Section 2. In particular, instead of denoting a fuzzy measure ψ we denote it by g and instead of denoting the criterion g we denote it directly by fuzzy set's membership function μ .

Fuzzy integrals that allow us to consider the interconnection of membership functions use a fuzzy measure. The fuzzy measure is a function $g : 2^R \to [0,1]$, where R is a set of some parameters that characterize some object. The fuzzy measure $g(Q_i)$ characterizes the total significance of parameters that are included in the set Q_i. The fuzzy measure satisfies the set of conditions [17]: specifically $g(\varnothing) = 0,\ g(Y) = 1$; if $Q, P \in Y$ and $Q \subset P$ then $g(Q) \le g(P)$.

If R is a set of all subsets of data sources subset $Y = \{Y_1, ..., Y_m\}$ then aggregation integrals can be put in as follows.

Fuzzy Sugeno integral: $A_k = A_k^S = \max\limits_{i=1}^{i=m}\ [\min(\mu_i^k, g(Q_i))]$,

where

$$\mu_1^k(y_1) \ge \mu_2^k(y_2) \ge ... \mu_m^k(y_m),\ Q_i = \{Y_1,...,\ Y_i\},\ i=1,...,m.$$

Fuzzy Choquet integral:

$$A_k = A_k^C = \sum_{i=1}^{i=m} [\mu_i^k(y_i) - \mu_{i+1}^k(y_{i+1})]g(Q_i),$$

where

$$\mu_1^k(y_1) \ge \mu_2^k(y_2) \ge ... \mu_m^k(y_m),\ Q_i = \{Y_1,...,\ Y_i\},\ i=1,...,m,\ \mu_{m+1}^k(y_{m+1})=0.$$

Fuzzy Choquet integral is usually interpreted as a generalization of the weighted arithmetic average notion and Sugeno integral as generalization of the weighted median concept (with aggregation of no less than three data sources). Due to their simplicity, the methods for calculation of the fuzzy measure based on the concept of g_λ-fuzzy measure introduced by Sugeno are very popular [6]. Fuzzy measure is called g_λ-fuzzy measure if the following condition is true for it: for all $Q, P \subset Y$ that $Q \cap P = \varnothing$ occurs $g(Q \cup P) = g(Q) + g(P) + \lambda g(Q)g(P)$ for some $\lambda > -1$.

Let's consider the procedure of the most popular method for g_λ-fuzzy measure calculation still labeling it as g.

Step 1. For each data source Y_i, $i=1,...,m$ select the value of fuzzy measure $g(Y_i) \in [0,1]$ as an importance degree of the data source Y_i. Values $g(Y_i)$ can be set by an expert, either being a result of an experiment or being received other way.

Step 2. Find a value λ using the equitation:

$$\lambda + 1 = \prod_{i=1}^{m} (1 + \lambda g(Y_i)).$$

Step 3. For all $Q_i = \{Y_1, ..., Y_i\}$, $i = 1, ..., m$ find recursive fuzzy measures $g(Q_i)$ using the following expressions:

$$g(Q_1) = g(Y_1) , g(Q_i) = g(Y_i) + g(Q_{i-1}) + \lambda g(Y_i) g(Q_{i-1}),$$
$$i = 2, ..., m.$$

Before considering a common procedure of fuzzy aggregation let's formalize the procedure of composition of the set Y_i and the procedure of recognition using the algorithm i with function $\mu(y_{ij_i})$. In general case the sources for aggregation are i algorithms, $i = 1, ..., m$ that use hidden information. In this section hidden information and the methods for their recognition are not considered. The things of interest are the results of the work of each algorithm as a source of a new separate signal $Y_i, i = 0, ..., m$ and a membership function $\mu(y_{ij_i}), y_{ij_i} \in Y_i, i = 0, ..., m, j_i = 0, ..., n_i$.

The main task of the procedure is aggregation of data sources $Y_i, i = 0, ..., m$. Each algorithm passes a preprocessing according to the next procedure 1 in order to form a set Y_i and membership functions $\mu(y_{ij_i}), y_{ij_i} \in Y_i, i = 0, ..., m, j_i = 0, ..., n_i$.

Step 1. A combination of empty sets $Y_i^k = \varnothing, k = 1, ..., K$ is specified.

Step 2. For each reference object k, $k = 1, ..., K$, a reference model $G_i^k, k = 1, ..., K$ is formed using the hidden information.

Step 3. Model G is formed for the recognizable object based on the same principles.

Step 4. Model G compared to each model $G_i^k, k = 1, ..., K$ resulting the calculation of the set of counts $\{y_i^1, y_i^2, ..., y_i^K\}$ which characterize the proximity of model G to models $G_i^k, k = 1, ..., K$ respectively.

Step 5. Sets $Y_i^k \cup y_i^k$, $k = 1,...,K$ are formed which are considered as new sets Y_i^k. If sets Y_i^k stop to change then go to step 6 (other criterions can be used to go to step 6). Else the procedure is started from step 2.

Step 6. Sets Y_i^k are joined resulting the set of $Y_i = \bigcup_{k=1}^{K} Y_i^k$ which is sorted (if it's numeral then the ascending sort is done) and its elements are indexed $i = 1,...,m$, $j_i = 0,...,n_i$ resulting a set $Y_i = \{ y_{ij_i} \in Y_i \mid i = 1,...,m, \; j_i = 0,...,n_i \}$. A membership function $\mu(y_{ij}), y_{ij} \in Y_i$, $i = 1,...,m, \; j = 0,...,n_i$ is specified on the set Y_i.

Recognition based on the separate algorithm i with function $\mu(y_{ij_i})$ can be done according to the following procedure 2.

Step 0. The forming of set Y_i and membership function $\mu(y_{ij_i}), y_{ij_i} \in Y_i, i = 0,...,m, \; j_i = 0,...,n_i$ is done with procedure 1.

Step 1. For each reference object k, $k = 1,...,K$ their own reference model is done using hidden information.

Step 2. Model G is formed for the recognizable object based on the same principles.

Step 3. Model G is compared with each model $G_i^k, k = 1,...,K$ resulting in a calculation of the set of counts $\{y_i^1, y_i^2,..., y_i^K\} \subset Y_i$ which characterize the proximity of model G to models $G_i^k, k = 1,...,K$ respectively.

Step 4. Model G is considered concurrent with that reference model G_i^k, the value $\mu(y_i^k), \; y_i^k \in Y_i$ being maximum for each one.

Thus the membership function $\mu(y_i^k), \; y_i^k \in Y_i$ estimates the proximity of the recognizable model to the corresponding reference model. The main task is fusion of data sources $Y_i, i = 1,...,m$ to increase the accuracy of recognition of user's activity.

Thus the common procedure 3 for aggregation of data sources using the Sugeno and the Choquet integrals will be done as follows.

Step 1. For each data source Y_i, $i = 1,...,m$ check the value $g(Y_i) \in [0,1]$ as an importance degree of data source Y_i.

Step 2. Find value λ using standard equation (defined in the previous section).

Step 3. Calculate a set of membership functions $\mu(y_i^k)$, $y_i^k \in Y_i$, $i = 1,...,m$ using procedure 2 for the recognizable object for each algorithm $i = 1,...,m$ and for each $k = 1,...,K$.

Step 4. For each $k = 1,...,K$ sort a set of functions $\mu(y_i^k)$ so $\mu(y_{j_1}^k) \geq \mu(y_{j_2}^k) \geq ... \geq \mu(y_{j_m}^k)$, $j_n \in \{1,...,m\}$.

Step 5. For each $k = 1,...,K$ calculate fuzzy measures values $g(Q_i^k)$ recursively, where $Q_i^k = \{Y_{j_1},..., Y_{j_i}\}$, $i = 1,...,m$ using recursive equation.

Step 6. Calculate fuzzy integral values $A_k = A_k^S$ (or $A_k = A_k^C$) for all $k = 1,...,K$. The recognizable object is considered concurrent with the reference object for which the value $A_k = A_k^S$ is maximum.

3.1.3. Method for Fuzzy Recognition of Users' Profiles

In general, each information set can contain L objects θ_l, $l = 1,...,L$ which are subject to recognition. Objects from different sets Θ_l can be in generally defined as r-nary relations $\Xi \in \Theta_{l_1} \times \Theta_{l_2} \times ... \times \Theta_{l_r}$, $\{l_1, l_2,..., l_r\} \subseteq \{1,..., L\}$.

Each of these relations Ξ we'll call the reference users' profile. By analogy with the recognizable object we'll identify the recognizable users' profile $\xi = < \theta_{l_1}, \theta_{l_2},... ,\theta_{l_r} >$, $\{l_1, l_2,..., l_r\} \subseteq \{1,..., L\}$, where $\theta_{l_1}, \theta_{l_2},...,\theta_{l_r}$ are the recognizable objects and the process of recognizing similarities with some reference users' profile Ξ we'll call the recognition of the profile ξ. The similarity of the recognized profile ξ with the reference profile Ξ characterized with the nonzero value of the similarity criterion we'll write as $\xi \approx \Xi$. In case the value of the similarity criterion is equal to zero then profile ξ is not similar to profile Ξ. This non-similarity is written this way $\xi \neq \Xi$.

Integral $A^j[\mu_1(y_1), \ \mu_2(y_2),..., \ \mu_m(y_m)]$ is used for calculation of the similarity of the recognizable θ and the reference object Θ^j. Membership functions $\mu_1(y_1), \ \mu_2(y_2),..., \ \mu_m(y_m)$ with values in the interval [0,1] are the arguments of this integral. Integral values also lie in the interval [0,1]. Thus, it is a function $[0,1]^m \to [0,1]$. Then, if for each object of the recognizable profile $\xi = <\theta_{l_1}, \ \theta_{l_2},... ,\theta_{l_r}>$ a set of criterion values $A_{l_1}, \ A_{l_2},..., \ A_{l_r}$ of its similarity with the objects $\Theta_{l_1}^{k_{l_1}}, \ \Theta_{l_2}^{k_{l_2}},..., \ \Theta_{l_r}^{k_{l_r}}$ of the reference profile is known then using some aggregation integral A we can calculate the similarity measure between the recognizable profile and the reference profile as a value of function $A[A_{l_1}, \ A_{l_2},..., \ A_{l_r}]$.

Procedure 4 of recognition of the separate profile $\xi = <\theta_{l_1}, \ \theta_{l_2},... ,\theta_{l_r}>$, $\{l_1, \ l_2,..., \ l_r\} \subseteq \{1,..., \ L\}$ that applies this idea will look as follows.

Step 1. Each object $\theta_{l_1}, \ \theta_{l_2},..., \theta_{l_r}$ is recognized separately comparing with reference objects $\Theta_{l_1}^{k_{l_1}}, \ \Theta_{l_2}^{k_{l_2}},..., \ \Theta_{l_r}^{k_{l_r}}$ $k_{l_r} = 1,..., \ K_{l_r}$, $\{l_1, \ l_2,..., \ l_r\} \subseteq \{1,..., \ L\}$ using fuzzy integrals $A_{l_1}, \ A_{l_2},..., \ A_{l_r}$. If for all recognizable objects $\theta_{l_1}, \ \theta_{l_2},..., \theta_{l_r}$ reference objects $\Theta_{l_1}^{\tilde{k}_1}, \ \Theta_{l_2}^{\tilde{k}_{l_2}},..., \ \Theta_{l_r}^{\tilde{k}_{l_r}}$ $\tilde{k}_{l_r} = 1,..., \ K_{l_r}$, similar to them were found such as

$\theta_{l_1} \approx \Theta_{l_1}^{\bar{k}_{l_1}}$, $\theta_{l_2} \approx \Theta_{l_2}^{\bar{k}_{l_2}}$,..., $\theta_{l_r} \approx \Theta_{l_r}^{\bar{k}_{l_r}}$ then go to step 2. If there was no

similar reference object found for at least one object θ_{l_1}, θ_{l_2},...,θ_{l_r} then go

to step 3.

Step 2. Profile $\xi = <\theta_{l_1}, \theta_{l_2},... ,\theta_{l_r}>$ is considered recognized

and similar to profile $\Xi = \Theta_{l_1}^{\bar{k}_{l_1}}, \Theta_{l_2}^{\bar{k}_{l_2}},..., \Theta_{l_r}^{\bar{k}_{l_r}}$ and the value of the

criterion for profile similarity is equal to $A[A_{l_1}^{\bar{k}_{l_1}}, A_{l_2}^{\bar{k}_{l_2}},..., A_{l_r}^{\bar{k}_{l_r}}]$.

Step 3. Profile $\xi = <\theta_{l_1}, \theta_{l_2},... ,\theta_{l_r}>$ was not recognized.

We'll call profiles $\Xi \in \Theta_{l_1} \times \Theta_{l_2} \times... \times \Theta_{l_r}$, $\{l_1, l_2,..., l_r\} \subseteq \{1,..., L\}$

the profiles of the 1st level and identify them Ξ_1. We'll call

profiles $\Xi_s \in \Xi_{s-1}^1 \times \Xi_{s-1}^2 \times... \times \Xi_{s-1}^v$ as profiles of the s-layer,

where $\Xi_{s-1}^1, \Xi_{s-1}^2,... ,\Xi_{s-1}^v$ are profiles of the $(s-1)$ layer. Thus the profiles

of the 1st layer are the relations of the objects and profiles of s-layer,

where $s > 1$ are relations of the profiles of $(s-1)$-layer. In order to recognize

$(s-j)$-level profiles ($j = 0, 1,..., s-2$) it is needed to recognize the profiles of

$(s-j-1)$-level which are related to $(s-j)$-level profiles. If during the

recognition of any $(s-j)$-level profile it is found that at least one $(s-j-1)$-

level profile included in the relation of this $(s-j)$-level profile can't be

recognized then the recognition process of the latter is stopped.

Development of the procedure 4 of the recognition of the 1st level

profiles can be put in the base of the method of s-layer profiles'

$\Xi_s \in \Xi_{s-1}^1 \times \Xi_{s-1}^2 \times... \times \Xi_{s-1}^v$ recognition as follows.

Step 1. Each object θ_{l_1}, θ_{l_2},...,θ_{l_r} that is included at least in one level

profile Ξ_1 is recognized by separate comparison with reference objects

$\Theta_{l_1}^{k_{l_1}}$, $\Theta_{l_2}^{k_{l_2}}$,..., $\Theta_{l_r}^{k_{l_r}}$ $k_{l_r} = 1,..., K_{l_r}$, $\{l_1, l_2,..., l_r\} \subseteq \{1,..., L\}$

using aggregation integrals A_{l_1}, A_{l_2},..., A_{l_r}.

Step 2. Each 1st level profile Ξ_1 for all objects which similar reference objects are found for is considered recognized and a similarity criterion is extracted for it (the value of the aggregation integral) A_1. After this go to step 3. If there was no such profiles found then there're no profiles of the first level and higher recognized and the execution is stopped.

Step 3. The value of level is set to 2 and we go to step 4.

Step 4. If s-level profiles Ξ_s were found for all $(s-1)$-level profiles of which non-zero values of the similarity criterion had been found then these profiles Ξ_s are considered recognized and similarity criteria (aggregation integral values) A_s are calculated for them. If there are any $(s+1)$-level profiles then step 4 is executed once again with the value $s = s+1$. Else the execution is stopped.

If no s-level profiles Ξ_s were found for all $(s-1)$-level profiles of which non-zero values of the similarity criterion had been found then there are no recognized s-level profiles and the execution is stopped.

3.1.4. Experiment

Error recognition or simply an error rate Pe is often the ultimate measure of the recognizer's accuracy. However, in many applications of pattern recognition, it is not sufficient to evaluate the performance of the classifier using only the error rate Pe, which determines the total number of system errors. In this case, we can use the following two concepts. False positives (Type I error) is the ratio of the number of pairs of identical user profiles that have not been found the system to the total number of compared pairs. False negatives (Type II error) are the ratios of the number of pairs of different user profiles which were found the same system to the total number of compared pairs. The Figures 2, 3 represent the diagram of values of the type II errors and the diagram of the stability values of the system (stability) which is equal to the difference of 100% and Type I errors.

Diagrams show that methods of recognition of users' profiles based on fuzzy clustering and Choquet and Sugeno aggregation operators have high stability. Moreover, the users' profiles recognition within the meta University network (mail, personal pages, sites, departments, «moodle» system, e-University) showed that the relevance of requests improved to 15% compared to the existing methods (EM clustering, fuzzy c-means, k-means) for a statistically significant sample of 1,500 queries on data related to more than 2,000 users.

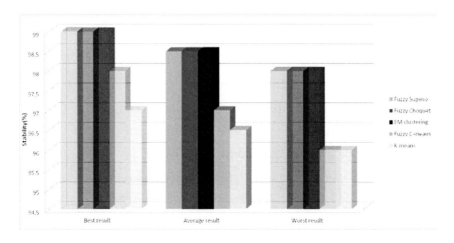

Figure 2. Stability of recognition of users' profiles.

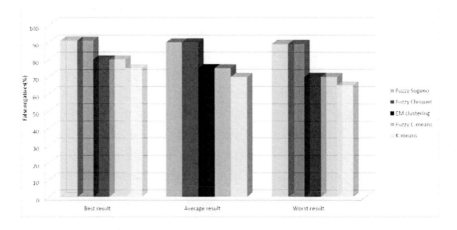

Figure 3. Type II error with the recognition of users' profiles.

3.2. The Method of Expert Knowledge Formalization about Web Pages Usability

In this section the method of expert knowledge formalization about web pages usability using fuzzy integral is considered. Also the problem of identification of fuzzy measures for aggregating user criteria is presented. Examples of assessments for 9 main usability criteria of web pages and results of web pages evaluation of 25 sites of leading universities in the world according QS ranking are provided.

3.2.1. Web Pages Usability Criteria

Only fifteen years ago for making a decision (in any field: choice of a vacation, shopping, cures for diseases, etc.) an individual usually relied on personal experience and information taken from various print sources as well as the experience of parents and friends. But at the beginning of new century, the main source of such information "de facto" became the Internet [57].

In the global network can be found web pages containing expert information varying degrees of competence and a large number of electronic versions of printed sources of varying quality. Therefore more acute become a question of professional assessment of usability and reliability of such sources of information in a global network. On the other hand, the user can formulate semantic criteria and their method of aggregation to create a generalized criterion for evaluating the properties of an information source to select the source on the basis of their preferences and intuitive senses [58, 59].

Thus, to evaluate the usability of information sources is an actual question related to the formalization of this assessment expertise. In this subsection the question of formalization of expertise in assessing the usability of web pages by aggregating user criteria using fuzzy aggregation operator Choquet (Choquet integral) is being reviewed. And by using this method the Universities' Usability Ranking of 25 best universities in the world is created.

User evaluation criteria of the usability of web pages can be formulated in different ways, depending on the purpose of the assessment and the particular expert [60]. Usually these criteria are divided into several groups [61]. From these criteria groups, in turn, in accordance with the logic of the expert a hierarchy can be constructed. Consider such a hierarchy and each of the criteria based on [62].

In order to achieve a simple and easy viewing a web page, it must meet several criteria: first, it is clear visual hierarchy of the page for the user, which denoted by G_1 . It includes the following several components (input criteria): g_1^1 - the degree of "isolated" or "underline" the most important elements on the page; g_2^1 - assessment of the condition "if the items are part of each other logically, they should be submitted as an attachment"; g_3^1 - degree of relatedness visual elements that are linked logically.

Second, utilization per page established conventions, general rules will be called G_2 . A criterion consists of two input criteria: g_1^2 - a clear indication of the active elements; g_2^2 - application of the standard notation and conventions (understandable in any language).

Third, the measure of separation of the web page to crisp the field for the user to comfortably navigate in these areas will be denoted G_3 . The criteria include the following components: g_1^3 - application of template "search, categories, content"; g_2^3 - the use of grid layout.

Fourth, the presence of visual noise, will be denoted G_4 . This criterion includes the following components: g_1^4 - measure "congestion" page elements; g_2^4 – the degree of presence of background noise. Figure 4 examples of known web pages are illustrated each of these criteria.

Figure 4. Examples of achieving a clear and easy viewing of Web pages: (a) g_1^1 - apple.com; (b) g_2^1 - tv.yandex.ru; (c) g_3^1 - vk.com; (d) g_1^2 - google.ru; (e) g_2^2 - progbook.com; (f) g_1^3 - lenta.ru; (g) g_2^3 - adidas.ru; (h) g_1^4 - iiis-summer13.org; (k) g_2^4 - letitbit-films.ru.

Consider the example of qualitative reasoning of the expert concerning the aggregation in given criteria. Obvious that some of these criteria are correlated, in particular G_1 and G_2.

Intuitively, if the web page has the property of clear visual hierarchy, then most likely, the designer has taken care of a good division of its contents on the crisp areas. Similarly, criteria g_1^2 and g_2^2 and correlated, since it is clear that if the web page is created with the use of the standard notation and conventions, it is likely that there are clearly marked on the active elements.

In accordance with the qualitative reasoning expert, if the web page is sufficiently possesses the property g_1^1, i.e., the most important elements are well marked and highlighted, in such circumstances, the criterion g_3^1 becomes more important to assess the clarity of visual hierarchy G_1, than the criterion g_2^1, since in this case the hyperlink "the most important element - its component parts" will be more user-friendly than visually unrelated, but adjacent to the selected element of its most important constituent parts. This phenomenon is known as the preferred dependence criteria. It is known [7] that no additive aggregation operators, including average, does not allow to formalize such expert arguments. In addition, the expert notes that in determining the presence of visual noise a measure of "congestion" page elements is more important than the degree of background noise presence.

Arguments of experts of such kind can be quite complex and ambiguous, depending on the particular expert opinion. For this reason, the formalization of expertise should allow experts to understand and correct the arguments of each other to end up with a coherent formal model. For this it is necessary to model allows one expert trace the chain of reasoning another expert and adjust it in accordance with its representation, arguing with all his adjustments. As a result of the joint work of the experts it is possible to get a consistent evaluation model. The process of its creation is iterative, each iteration in this case will be "making reasonable amendments" one or another expert.

3.2.2. Fuzzy Measure and Integral in Web Usability Evaluation

Aggregation operator is often referred to possess certain desired properties function of the H variables (criteria), each of which is defined on the unit interval. The range of values of this function is also a unit interval. In accordance with this aggregation operator denote the $A:[0,1]^H \rightarrow [0,1]$, where H - the criteria [8]. Thus, for the formalization of expertise, discussed in the previous subsection, it is necessary to find a suitable operator $A(g_1^1,...,g_3^1,g_1^2,g_2^2,g_1^3,g_2^3,g_1^4,...,g_3^4)$. The result of aggregation using this operator will be estimate of the usability (Ω) of a web page in the interval [0,1]. With the help of this evaluation it will be possible to rank pages according to their usability. In this sense, the difference is more important in the evaluation of individual pages than the absolute value of this estimate.

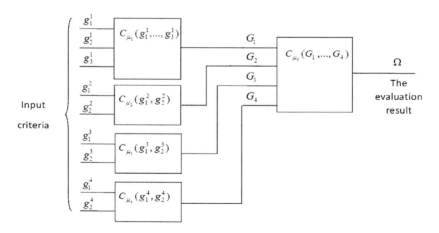

Figure 5. Tree of Choquet integrals to evaluate the usability of a web page.

For working with the criteria on the unit scale normalization of all necessary criteria is necessary. For example, if the assessment of the relevant web pages to different criteria is set in accordance with a scale

{0,1, ..., 9.10}, the normalization of the scale will result in the scale {0,0.1, ..., 0.9,1} and will consist in dividing each possible evaluation at 10. If different criteria for evaluation are used different scales, these scales must be reduced to a single segment (normalized).

The most suitable from a practical point of view is the use of 2-order Choquet integral, because it allows to formalize the expert arguments, such as those described in the previous section, while remaining simple enough [21]. In accordance with the hierarchy of considered criteria it is possible to construct a tree of 2-order Choquet integrals [63, 64]. The corresponding structure is a "nested" into each other Choquet integrals (Figure 5).

Figure 5 shows all listed in the previous section the input criteria and the criteria for the components, which are themselves the results of aggregation of the input criteria. Choquet integrals $C_{\mu_1}(g_1^1,...g_3^1), C_{\mu_2}(g_1^2,g_2^2), C_{\mu_3}(g_1^3,g_2^3), C_{\mu_4}(g_1^4,g_2^4)$ are used to obtain the values of the constituent criteria $G_1,...,G_4$. The integral $C_{\mu_5}(G_1,...,G_4)$ needs to aggregate all the constituent criteria. The result of the assessment is the value of this integral obtained by the values of the input criteria for a particular web page. Express the result of the evaluation by the corresponding integrals Choquet:

$$\Omega = C_{\mu_5}(C_{\mu_1}(g_1^1,...g_3^1), C_{\mu_2}(g_1^2,g_2^2), C_{\mu_3}(g_1^3,g_2^3), C_{\mu_4}(g_1^4,g_2^4)) \qquad (3)$$

3.2.3. Example of Expert Knowledge Formalization

Today more and more popular become university sites that are accessed by multiple audiences: applicants for information on admission, students for orientation in university events and professors who are looking for background information [65-68]. For example, according to the statistics: bmstu.ru is visited every day up to 15 thousand users. Accordingly, any discomfort or inconvenience caused by the user when interacting with the site leads to the translation of these emotions on the assessment of the University as a whole for thousands of people every day. An order of magnitude, this value increases to sites of leading universities in the world. Therefore consider the presented fuzzy method for the initial web pages of the leading universities (rated QS). To simplify, the main operations of the method will be considered on the example of three universities: Massachusetts Institute of Technology (MIT) - web.mit.edu, Cambridge University (CU) - cam.ac.uk and Harvard University (HU) - harvard.edu (Figure 6).

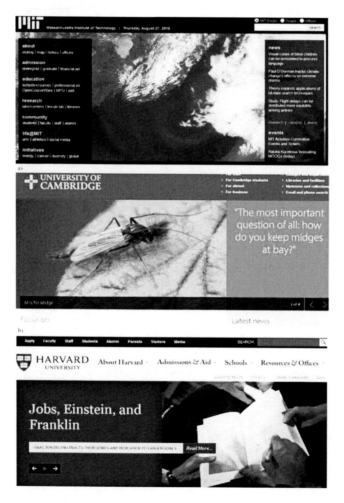

Figure 6. The initial web pages of leading universities in the world: (a) MIT - web.mit.edu; (b) CU - cam.ac.uk; (c) HU - harvard.edu.

For the formation of a statistically representative sample of the algorithm for stratification were selected evaluating web pages of these sites on a 10-point scale, 75 students enrolled at the undergraduate chair of Bauman University. In accordance to this algorithm, the sample consisted of grade ratings made up by students who have been selected as follows. Of educational groups of students was drawn up a common list. After error checking and no of repeatability was selected every third item. Then each selected student assessed, thus forming a sample of the resulting estimates. The evaluation results, which were carried out on the basic rules of usability testing [69], are presented in Table 3.1.

Table 3.1. The values of the criteria for the test sites

Input criteria	CU (g_1)	MIT (g_2)	HU (g_3)
g_1^1	0.3	0.9	0.9
g_2^1	0.7	0.7	0.5
g_3^1	0.4	0.5	0.7
g_1^2	0.6	0.6	0.6
g_2^2	0.6	0.9	0.9
g_1^3	0.4	0.8	0.9
g_2^3	0.4	0.9	0.8
g_1^4	0.2	0.8	0.8
g_2^4	0.3	0.8	0.9

Despite the leadership among universities, the first criterion for CU estimated as very low, when the MIT and HU level of indication of the most important elements on the page was quite decent. The degree of visual coherence of elements g_2^1 was evaluated quite satisfactorily for all sites. Nesting of elements g_3^1 is not the determining criterion for this type of sites, so its average value. All three universities excelled in using standard notation and conventions g_1^2, of course taking into account the specialties to which the they are focused. Despite the visual similarity techniques used for constructing web pages, clear criterion for designation of active elements was valued almost as much as possible in MIT and HU, and a little less at CU. All sites use user interface template "search, categories, content," but just for CU, the criterion has a relatively small value, possibly because of poor color solutions, while not directly test of "color" is not considered here. It may be noted that in general, the criteria for dividing web pages into distinct area g_2^3 in particular has a maximum value at the site of the HU. The most overloaded page g_1^4 is a web page at CU. In addition, the experts did not satisfy the level of background noise g_2^4 at the CU's site. The experts were also asked about the overall assessment of the usability of each of the web pages. For experts it was obvious that the MIT and HU sites are more comfortable than the CU site what can be formalized in the form of the following preference relations:

$$\mathbf{g}_2 \succ_{\mu_5} \mathbf{g}_1 \tag{4}$$

$$\mathbf{g}_3 \succ_{\mu_5} \mathbf{g}_1 \tag{5}$$

Here $\mathbf{g}_1, ..., \mathbf{g}_3$ - the implementation of the input criteria for sites CU, MIT and HU. Index μ_5 means that the preference relation considered as part of the final assessment, which is formed by integral $C_{\mu_5}(G_1, ..., G_4)$. Other preferences are not so obvious to the experts. Taking into account the above qualitative considerations one of the experts regarding the impact on the result of the criteria $g_1^1, ..., g_3^1$, the experts came to the conclusion that the assessment for the HU site must be higher than ratings for MIT site what can express a preference relation:

$$\mathbf{g}_3 \succ_{\mu_5} \mathbf{g}_2 \tag{6}$$

Positive correlation criteria G_1 and G_2, as well as a positive correlation criteria g_1^2 and g_2^2 is formalized by the sign corresponding indexes interaction criteria:

$$I_{\mu_5}(1,2) < 0 \tag{7}$$

$$I_{\mu_2}(1,2) < 0 \tag{8}$$

Here the indices μ_5 and μ_2 means that the interaction indexes of criteria refer to Choquet integrals on fuzzy measure μ_5 and μ_2 respectively. Given above expert' arguments that in determining the presence of visual noise G_4, g_1^4 is more important - a measure of "congestion" page elements than g_2^4 - the degree of presence of background noise, formalized by means of appropriate Shapley indices:

$$\Phi_{\mu_4}(1) > \Phi_{\mu_4}(2) \tag{9}$$

Here the μ_4 index means that the Shapley index refers to the Choquet integral for fuzzy measure μ_4. In addition, when evaluating the visual clarity hierarchy expert pointed dependence preferred criteria $g_1^1, ..., g_3^1$. This phenomenon is formalized by the following relation of preference:

$$\mathbf{g}_3 \succ_{\mu_1} \mathbf{g}_2 \tag{10}$$

Index μ_1 here indicates that the preference relation is considered in the framework of local evaluation of criterion G_1, formed by an integral $C_{\mu_1}(g_1^1, \ldots g_3^1)$.

3.2.4. Identification of Fuzzy Measures

In order to get the result in accordance with (3) it is necessary to identify fuzzy measure $\mu_1, \ldots, \mu_5$ on the basis of expert preferences expressed by constraints (4-10). For the identification method was chosen to maximize the entropy of fuzzy measures under given constraints [30]. This method is based on the principle proposed in [31]. This principle is that if there are some part of the knowledge about the behavior of a random variable, then to that part of knowledge that is not available, should be treated with the most unbiased, maximizing the entropy of this magnitude, taking into account existing knowledge. In [29] was proposed to apply this principle for the identification of fuzzy measures. As a result, it can be obtained the least specific fuzzy measure of all possible under the constraints imposed by the expert preferences. In accordance with the method of entropy maximization preference relation (4-6) are translated into inequality:

$$C_{\mu_5}(C_{\mu_1}(0.9, 0.7, 0.5), C_{\mu_2}(0.6, 0.9), C_{\mu_3}(0.8, 0.9), C_{\mu_4}(0.8, 0.8)) -$$
$$C_{\mu_5}(C_{\mu_1}(0.3, 0.7, 0.4), C_{\mu_2}(0.6, 0.6), C_{\mu_3}(0.4, 0.4), C_{\mu_4}(0.2, 0.3)) \geq \delta_C^{\mu_5} \tag{11}$$

$$C_{\mu_5}(C_{\mu_1}(0.9, 0.5, 0.7), C_{\mu_2}(0.6, 0.9), C_{\mu_3}(0.9, 0.8), C_{\mu_4}(0.8, 0.8)) -$$
$$C_{\mu_5}(C_{\mu_1}(0.3, 0.7, 0.4), C_{\mu_2}(0.6, 0.6), C_{\mu_3}(0.4, 0.4), C_{\mu_4}(0.2, 0.3)) \geq \delta_C^{\mu_5} \tag{12}$$

$$C_{\mu_5}(C_{\mu_1}(0.9, 0.5, 0.7), C_{\mu_2}(0.6, 0.9), C_{\mu_3}(0.9, 0.8), C_{\mu_4}(0.8, 0.8)) -$$
$$C_{\mu_5}(C_{\mu_1}(0.9, 0.7, 0.5), C_{\mu_2}(0.6, 0.9), C_{\mu_3}(0.8, 0.9), C_{\mu_4}(0.8, 0.8)) \geq \delta_C^{\mu_5} \tag{13}$$

Inequality (7-9) are converted, respectively, in the inequality:

$$-1 \leq I_{\mu_5}(1,2) \leq -\delta_I^{\mu_5} \tag{14}$$

$$-1 \leq I_{\mu_2}(1,2) \leq -\delta_I^{\mu_2} \tag{15}$$

$$\Phi_{\mu_4}(1) - \Phi_{\mu_4}(2) \geq \delta_\Phi^{\mu_4} \tag{16}$$

Preference relation (10) is transferred to the inequality:

$$C_{\mu_1}(0.9, 0.5, 0.7) - C_{\mu_1}(0.9, 0.7, 0.5) \geq \delta_C^{\mu_1} \tag{17}$$

Here $\delta_C^{\mu_1}, \delta_C^{\mu_5}, \delta_I^{\mu_2}, \delta_I^{\mu_5}, \delta_\Phi^{\mu_4}$ - indifference thresholds defined by expert for the identification of fuzzy measures. Based on a fact that all the input criteria defined on the scales of the form {0,0.1, ..., 0.9,1}, as well as taking into account the restrictions on the indifference thresholds, used to prevent the selection of the thresholds at which obviously has no solutions of fuzzy measures identification problem, measures $\mu_1, ..., \mu_4$ were chosen for the following values of these thresholds: $\delta_C^{\mu_1} = 0.055$, $\delta_I^{\mu_2} = 0.005$, $\delta_\Phi^{\mu_4} = 0.02$. For the measure μ_5 given the limitations and inequalities (11-14) were selected thresholds $\delta_C^{\mu_5} = 0.03$, $\delta_I^{\mu_5} = 0.0027$.

For the identification of fuzzy measures $\mu_1, ..., \mu_5$ was used specialized Kappalab package [27]. In the first phase measures $\mu_1, ..., \mu_4$ have been identified on the basis of constraints (15-17). The results of this identification in the form of parameters of the corresponding integrals (interaction indices and Shapley indices) as well as the values of these integrals on realizations $\mathbf{g}_1, \mathbf{g}_2, \mathbf{g}_3$ are shown in Table. 3.2 in the respective columns. At the second stage also by the method of maximizing the entropy of fuzzy measure μ_5 has been identified on the basis of imposed restrictions (11-14) and received on the first stage of the integrals $C_{\mu_1}, ..., C_{\mu_4}$. Table. 3.2 on the bottom line shows the parameters and the value of the integral C_{μ_5} on the implementations $\mathbf{g}_1, \mathbf{g}_2, \mathbf{g}_3$.

As expected, these values (results of aggregation) reflect expert usability evaluations of relevant web pages formulated in the form of preference relations (4-6) and then translated into inequality (11-13). Negative interaction (correlation) criteria G_1 and G_2 (5), marked by expert, expressed a negative interaction index $I_{\mu_5}(1,2)$. Correlation criteria g_1^2 and g_2^2 (6) are expressed in a negative interaction index $I_{\mu_5}(1,2)$. The difference in the subjective "weight" criteria g_1^4 and g_2^4 (7) reflects the corresponding values of the Shapley indices $\Phi_{\mu_4}(1)$ и $\Phi_{\mu_4}(2)$. Preferred dependence of criteria $g_1^1, ..., g_3^1$ reflected in the results of the identification value of the integral C_{μ_1} on the realizations $\mathbf{g}_1, \mathbf{g}_2, \mathbf{g}_3$. Thus, in the identification of fuzzy measures $\mu_1, ..., \mu_5$ covering all the expert preferences. The coefficients of these measures are the parameters for the respective integrals, which, in turn, form a tree evaluation.

3.2.5. Universities' Usability Ranking

Table 3.3 presents the results of usability testing of leading universities' web sites using the fuzzy method. In the first column the QS ranking of university is represented. The second column contains the name of the university, the country of the university is in the third column. The fourth column contains information about QS mark of the university. In the next column the normalized usability mark of the university is given. The sixth column shows how many positions of the ranking the university shifted depending on the result of usability mark. Finally the new usability ranking of the university and its name is presented.

Table 3.2. Parameters and values of the Choquet integrals

Choquet integrals	Parameters									
	$\Phi(1)$	$\Phi(2)$	$\Phi(3)$	$\Phi(4)$	$I(1,2)$	$I(2,3)$	$I(1,3)$	g_1	g_2	g_3
C_{μ_1}	0.333	0.247	0.419	-	-0.103	0	0.103	0.456	0.672	0.727
C_{μ_2}	0.5	0.5	-	-	-0.005	-	-	0.6	0.750	0.750
C_{μ_3}	0.5	0.5	-	-	0	-	-	0.4	0.85	0.85
C_{μ_4}	0.51	0.49	-	-	0	-	-	0.249	0.8	0.849
C_{μ_5}	0.267	0.234	0.234	0.264	-0.002	-0.004	0.029	0.425	0.763	0.793

Table 3.3. Universities' usability ranking

QS ranking	University	Country	QS mark	Usability mark	Shift	Usability ranking	University
1	California Institute of Technology	United States	94,9	8,80	↑0	1	California Institute of Technology
2	Harvard University	United States	93,9	8,10	↓7	1	University of Oxford
2	University of Oxford	United Kingdom	93,9	8,80	↑1	2	University of Michigan
4	Stanford University	United States	93,8	6,90	↓13	3	University of Pennsylvania
5	Massachusetts Institute of Technology	United States	93	8,20	↓2	4	Cornell University
6	Princeton University	United States	92,7	6,88	↓12	5	ETH Zürich – Swiss Federal Institute of Technology Zürich
7	University of Cambridge	United Kingdom	92,3	7,72	↓4	6	Massachusetts Institute of Technology
8	University of California, Berkeley	United States	89,8	7,34	↓7	7	Imperial College London
9	University of Chicago	United States	87,8	7,38	↓5	8	Harvard University
10	Imperial College London	United Kingdom	87,5	8,20	↑2	9	Carnegie Mellon University
11	Yale University	United States	87,4	6,63	↓11	10	University of Cambridge
12	University of California, Los Angeles	United States	86,3	6,60	↓11	11	Northwestern University

Table 3.3. (Continued)

QS ranking	University	Country	QS mark	Usability mark	Shift	Usability ranking	University
13	Columbia University	United States	85,2	6,78	↓6	12	University of Washington
14	ETH Zürich – Swiss Federal Institute of Technology Zürich	Switzer-land	84,5	8,24	↑8	13	University of Chicago
15	Johns Hopkins University	United States	83,7	6,65	↓6	14	University of California, Berkeley
16	University of Pennsylvania	United States	81	8,44	↑12	15	University of Toronto
17	Duke University	United States	79,3	6,48	↓6	16	Stanford University
18	University of Michigan	United States	79,2	8,48	↑16	17	Princeton University
19	Cornell University	United States	79,1	8,32	↑14	18	Columbia University
20	University of Toronto	Canada	78,3	7,10	↑4	19	University College London
21	University College London	United Kingdom	77.6	6,77	↑1	20	Johns Hopkins University
22	Northwestern University	United States	77,1	7,52	↑10	21	Yale University
23	The University of Tokyo	Japan	76,4	6,16	↓2	22	University of California, Los Angeles
24	Carnegie Mellon University	United States	76	8,00	↑14	23	Duke University
25	University of Washington	United States	73,4	7,42	↑12	24	The University of Tokyo

Analyzing the table one can notes that two best universities saved their leading positions: California Institute of Technology, University of Oxford. But other universities from the beginning of QS ranking do not actually accent on usability of web interface that presents an organization in the Internet. In general, results confirm the popular belief that there is no direct correlation between the level of the university and the usability of its web site [70], and results also confirm that the academic web sites do not always keep to basic principles of human-computer interaction [71, 72].

3.3. The Method of Determining the Weights in Information Retrieval Using the Fuzzy Choquet Integral

3.3.1. Information Retrieval Based on Weighted Zone Scoring

Information retrieval based on weighted zone scoring means the assignment weight for each zone or each field in the document metadata [73]. All these weights are usually obtained using machine learning methods. The subsection presents a method of determining the weights using the fuzzy Choquet integral. This method allows one to take into account possible interdependence between the zone parameters when calculating the relevance and to obtain higher scoring accuracy.

Information retrieval is the search for documents which are relevant to the text query using various techniques [74, 75]. When working with large collections of documents the search results can be so big that the user will simply not be able to see them all. So one of the important tasks of information retrieval is to rank search results according to their relevance to the query.

If we use the documents' metadata in this ranking we need to take into account the expert's knowledge about metadata's structure and its characteristics. Documents' metadata are the fields (such as the date the document was created, type of document, the book's cost, etc.) and the zones (title, author, publisher, abstract, keywords, the text etc.). The difference between the zones and fields lies in the fact that the field may have a limited predefined set of values and the zone's set of values is not limited. Further we consider the fields as a special case of zones. Search results ranking method is very detailed described in [73]. This method is based on allocating weight w_h to each zone h. The weights are setting using machine learning based on training examples. Denote the text query as q and the document as d. In weighted zone scoring each pair (q, d) is assigned a value on the unit interval by calculating the linear combination of each zone scores. Consider a set of documents each of which has H zones. Let $w_h \in [0, 1]$, $1 \le h \le H$ such that $\sum_{h=1}^{H} w_h = 1$, $s_h \in [0,1]$, while zone score s_h considering the degree of compliance (or non) between the query and the h-th zone of the document. This value can be calculated in different ways for each of the zones [73]. Consider one of the most common ways to calculate it. For example, if all the query terms contained in the particular zone, value s_h is equal to 1; if only one term is contained in the zone, value s_h is equal to 1/r; if any term is not contained in the zone, value s_h is equal to zero, where r is the number of terms in the query. Other ways to compute this value involve using the frequency with which the query term occurs in the particular zone as input information or may be based on quality indicators of the document, age of the document, its length and so on. In particular, there is a classic zone score calculating method based on the band function BM25F [76], which takes into account the query term occurrence frequency in the document zones. BM25F is based on function BM25 [77] which is a linear combination of three main attributes: the term frequency, the document frequency, and the length of the document. In this section, the focus is made not on how to calculate the zone scores s_h but on the aggregation of these scores into a single score of document's relevance to the query $score(q,d)$. This aggregation is performed by a linear combination of zone scores [73]:

$$score(q,d) = \sum_{h=1}^{H} w_h s_h \qquad (18)$$

Suppose that we have a set of training examples each of which is a tuple consisting of the query q, the document d, and rating of relevance for the pair (q, d). Usually each query q is linked with a set of documents which is completely ordered by an expert according to their relevance. In accordance to this order the rating of relevance can be assigned by the expert within unit's interval. Then the weights w_h are determined by machine learning using available examples so that the resulting values of the weights allow to approximate the rating of relevance of the training examples. Getting weight coefficients is reduced to an optimization problem with the objective function in the form of total error corresponding to training examples. There are also empirical rules for weights assigning to the document zones. For example, the authors of paper [78] believe that they can achieve higher ranking accuracy by assigning the relatively high weight to the document title zone. The paper [79] made the assumption that the ranking accuracy of news' documents can be increased by separating the first sentence to a separate zone and assigning increased weight to this zone. These and other similar rules can be applied in machine learning within the zone scores aggregation using a weighted arithmetic mean aggregation operator [80].

The approach described above in all its varieties assumes an implicit assumption of the mutual independence of the values s_i. However, it can be shown that the values s_i can be dependent of each other. For example, if the query term is in the title of the news' document most likely to meet this term in the first sentence of the document. In this case, we are dealing with a positive correlation between values s_i and if we calculate the relevance score by a weighted arithmetic mean (18) we obviously get some redundancy of result. This phenomenon of aggregated values positive correlation and ways of compensation corresponding redundancy to the result is discussed in detail for example in [27]. A possible example of a more complex dependence will be the next one. Suppose an expert knows the following: query term occurs both in the body and in the abstract of several documents. These documents are ordered by relevance using the following rule. The document with the same term in the head zone is more relevant to the query than document with the same term in the "document type" zone. Such dependence between the zone scores S_i is known as the preferred dependence of criteria [27]. This dependence cannot be expressed by any of the additive operators including the weighted arithmetic mean operator. Such knowledge cannot be formalized by the form of rules for the zones' weights obtaining using machine learning with weighted average aggregation operators. Thus, we round off the result when applying the weighted average operator to compute the relevance of documents to the query and assuming that the values S_i are always independent of each other.

3.3.2. Fuzzy Measure and the Choquet Integral in Weighted Zone Scoring

If we use the weighted arithmetic mean operator for weighted zone scoring then weights W_h can be directly set by the expert. But due to the great complexity of this task in most cases these weights are determined based on machine learning [73].

In [81-83] discussed in detail the application of a new method of machine learning based on the Choquet integral in different application areas, and concluded the feasibility of its use. In the field of information retrieval Choquet integral can be used for modeling expert preferences formalized by rules similar to the rules described in the previous section.

If we use the Choquet integral for weighted zone scoring it is required to obtain a fuzzy measure ψ instead of weights W_h. Direct assignment of fuzzy measure by an expert is even more difficult task than weights setting due to exponentially increasing complexity. For example, for the ten criteria an expert will have to set $2^{10} = 1024$ fuzzy measure's coefficients. Such setting is impossible in practice. Therefore, the coefficients of fuzzy measure ψ are obtained using machine learning as it is done for the weighted arithmetic mean operator. For realization of such machine learning procedure it is necessary to form a set of training examples and a set of formal empirical rules like those described above. Each of the training examples is a triple $\Delta_k = (d_k, \ q_k, \ r(q_k, \ d_k))$ in which the assessment of relevance $r(q_k, \ d_k)$ of the document d_k to the query q_k is assigned by an expert on the unit interval or these assessments are ranked by an expert. The rules are the limitations both on the fuzzy measure and the Choquet integral as weak partial orders on the set of zone scores realizations, results of aggregation (final relevance of the document), the Shapley indices, and interaction indices of criteria. Methods used to formalize these rules are considered in detail in [27]. In particular, if the rule states that the zone scores are correlated then it will be formalized by assigning a positive sign to the interaction index of these scores. In practice, to enable the expert to create such rules it is common to use 2nd-order fuzzy measures and, accordingly, 2nd-order Choquet integrals. Remaining relatively simple it allows to model the interaction between the criteria which are described by the rules similar to the above-mentioned (as it noted above, in the paper [22] we can find conditions under which such a simplification (using of the 2-order Choquet integral) is correct). For each training example, we have the s_h values that are appropriated for any area of the document. Relevance of the document d_k to the query q_k will be determined as $score(q_k, \ d_k) = C_\psi(s_1, ..., \ s_H)$. Because of the nature of available information in the form of rules described above we need to choose a method of identification of fuzzy measure.

One of the advantages of fuzzy measure identification method based on minimization of fuzzy measure variance is the lack of any strict requirements to input information, in contrast to other methods of identification of fuzzy measure. This method is based on the principle of maximum entropy [14]. We will follow this principle in weighted zone scoring of the documents, that is, taking into account the expert knowledge in the form of training examples and rules we will consider the missing information without bias.

3.3.3. The Procedure for Determining the Weights for Weighted Zone Scoring

If the aggregation operator is the Choquet integral with respect to the fuzzy measure, this procedure consists of the following steps.

Step 1. Form a set of zones $J = \{1,..., H\}$ for the document and a method of zone scores s_h calculating.

Step 2. Generate training examples using a collection of documents, these examples being relevance estimation and (or) non-strict partial order on the set of the estimates, i.e., implement expert ranking of documents relative to the query. Create rules in the form of partial weak orders on sets of Choquet integral parameters.

Step 3. Formalize obtained on the previous step information in the form of restrictions on the Choquet integral parameters in the form of inequalities with indifference thresholds. Set the indifference thresholds from training examples and scales that have been applied.

Step 4. Identify fuzzy measure on the basis of obtained in the previous step information by the minimizing dispersion method.

When new available information is added to the set of training examples and the set of rules the procedure is repeated from step 3. The Choquet integral with respect to the fuzzy measure ψ is aggregating operator for zone scores s_h through which the documents are ranked according to their relevance to the query.

3.3.4. Experiment

During the experiment we do not attempt to create a complete search engine. The purpose of experimental study was to obtain an answer to the question about the practical applicability of fuzzy measures and the

Choquet integral in the field of information retrieval for weighted zone scoring.

A set of training examples included 30 queries, 100 terms, and 300 documents (publications in the field of artificial intelligence).

The procedure discussed above was put in practice to determine the fuzzy measures for the weighted zone scoring.

Step 1. We considered five zones of document: title $(h = 1)$, abstract $(h = 2)$, keywords $(h = 3)$, main text $(h = 4)$, and references $(h = 5)$.

These zones correspond to the zone indicators s_h which are calculated based on the function BM25F [76].

Step 2. Initial data for machine learning comprised both set of training examples and the following empirical rules similar to those discussed above.

Set of training examples Δ_k, where $k = 1,\ldots,$ 1000 was received with experts' support. As noted above, each of these examples is a triple: $\Delta_k = (q_k, d_k, r(q_k, d_k))$. Relevance of the document d_k to the query q_k was evaluated on a scale which is the set S={0, 1, 2, 3, 4} in the same manner as it was done in [80]. In this set, "0" means that the document does not fully matches the query (no relevance), "4" means full compliance (document is relevant to the query), other values correspond to intermediate gradations of relevance.

Also, we obtained the following empirical rules in this step with experts' support:

Rule 1. If the query term was met in the title, it is likely to meet the same term both in the abstract and in the main text.

This rule means that the corresponding criteria are positively correlated and their interaction indices are less than zero. Then interaction indices of these criteria are defined by the following inequalities:

$$I(1,3) < 0; \quad I(1,4) < 0; \quad I(3,4) < 0 \tag{19}$$

Rule 2. In order to have the document relevant to the query it is least important that the query term is contained in the list of references; more importantly, that the query term is contained in the main text; more importantly to meet the term in the keywords; and finally, most importantly to meet the query term in the title and (or) in the annotation.

This rule means the following. Importance of the criterion s_5 is less than the importance of the criterion s_4. Similarly, importance of the criterion s_4 is less than importance of the criterion s_3. Importance of the criterion s_1 is the same as importance of the criterion s_2 and more than importance of the criterion s_3. This reasoning can be expressed by a partial weak order $\succeq_J$ on the set J of document's zones:

$$5 \prec_J 4 \prec_J 2 \prec_J 1 \sim_J 3 \tag{20}$$

Rule 3. If the query term is found in the main text and in the abstract, in order to get the document being more relevant to the query it is preferable that the same term is contained in the title rather than it is contained in the "keywords." This rule can be expressed by the following preference relations on the set S of available realizations of criteria:

$$\mathbf{s}_1 \prec_S \mathbf{s}_2$$
$$\mathbf{s}_3 \prec_S \mathbf{s}_2$$

Here $\mathbf{s}_1$, $\mathbf{s}_2$, $\mathbf{s}_3$ are the realizations of criteria for three documents from the training set.

Step 3. Inequalities (19) are translated into inequalities with indifference thresholds:

$$-\delta_I < I(1,3) < 0; \quad -\delta_I < I(1,4) < 0; \quad \delta_I < I(3,4) < 0$$

Here δ_I - indifference threshold defined by an expert. This threshold is interpreted as minimum significantly non-zero absolute value of interaction index.

Partial weak order (20) is translated into inequalities with Shapley indexes of the criteria:

$$\Phi_{Sh}(4) - \Phi_{Sh}(5) \geq \delta_{Sh}; \quad \Phi_{Sh}(2) - \Phi_{Sh}(4) \geq \delta_{Sh};$$
$$\Phi_{Sh}(1) - \Phi_{Sh}(2) \geq \delta_{Sh}; \quad \Phi_{Sh}(3) - \Phi_{Sh}(2) \geq \delta_{Sh};$$
$$-\delta_{Sh} \leq \Phi_{Sh}(3) - \Phi_{Sh}(1) \leq \delta_{Sh}$$

Here δ_{Sh} is the indifference threshold defined by an expert. Shapley indices are significantly distinguished if their absolute difference exceeds indifference threshold δ_{Sh}.

Step 4. Training examples and rules formed the restrictions imposed on the Choquet integral and its parameters during the identification process of fuzzy measures. Fuzzy measure was identified by the minimum variance method using specialized package Kappalab [27] in accordance with the above described optimization problem. An important question that arose in the identification process related to the need for expert's assignment of indifference thresholds. These values were chosen on the basis of the document relevance scale: for the aggregation result indifference threshold was taken to be $\delta_c = 0,25$. In addition, restrictions imposed on the indifference thresholds have been met (these thresholds can be set so that the fuzzy measure identification problem obviously does not have a solution), thus inequality proposed in [26] constraints the implementation of which allows one to exclude such a situation.

Experiments for evaluating the accuracy of proposed method were performed on a statistically significant sample of 500 search queries containing the terms of training examples in various combinations.

Initially we calculated the documents' relevance $score(q_k, d_k)$ to these search queries using the set of training examples Δ_k , the empirical rules 1-3, and the method described above.

Then we calculated the relevance $score(q_k, d_k)$ on the basis of the machine learning method described in [73] and the set of training examples Δ_k .

Finally, it was found that the accuracy of search results ranking when using 2nd order Choquet integral aggregation has improved by an average of 4.5% when compared to the weighted average aggregation operator. The ranking accuracy considered is the difference between the relevance assigned by an expert and document relevance prepared on the basis of weighted zone scoring aggregation with one of two aggregation operators considered in this section.

CONCLUSION

The chapter considers the practical applications of fuzzy measure and the fuzzy integral and analyzes the problems in these applications. The main barrier on a way of wide practical use of these tools is related to the problems of the expert knowledge formalization in the form of fuzzy measure coefficients. It seems possible to overcome these difficulties by using methods of visualization adapted for each separate area of practical applications. Therefore a field of research related to data fusion based on fuzzy measures and integrals is developing intensively.

The method that uses fuzzy aggregation and recognition with fuzzy measures and integrals for Web personalization was considered in Subsection 3.1. Application of the suggested method can be useful when there is no other method to deploy a complete ontology or a semantic network of the company but there are a lot of tools for electronic communication and interaction created. The main advantages and differences of the method from the analogs are:

- The ability to consider the measure of importance of each data source during the process of hierarchic recognition due to usage of both aggregation integrals that use a fuzzy measure.
- The ability to increase the accuracy of recognition of users' profiles using all stages for the personalization starting from aggregation of a single user's query and ending with individual users' profiles.
- Promising opportunities for development of intellectual and intuitive human-computer interaction by using more data sources and related items.

The Subsection 3.2. discusses the method of formalization of expert knowledge about the usability of web pages. In human-computer interaction one can single out two components: human and computer. And despite the considerable number of philosophical, cultural and socio-psychological theories it is the human component remains the most difficult to systematize. Under the assumption that the methods of technical university, consisting of a formal description of processes and particularly human-computer interaction with web pages are an effective tool in solving this problem. The fuzzy integral as a modern and logically confirmable fuzzy tool with respect to fuzzy measure was used for this purpose. Results of experimental research of universities' usability obtained with fuzzy method correspond to the current HCI trends that also confirms the adequacy of the proposed method. In general, method can be used in wide ergonomic field of expert knowledge formalization. In continuation of this work is planned to expand the experimental research through the software automation of this technique as an annex to the several universities web sites.

The Subsection 3.3. considers the practical application of fuzzy measure and the fuzzy integral in the field of information retrieval.

Experimental results have shown that increasing the accuracy of documents' relevance ranking can be achieved by using the fuzzy integral as an aggregation operator for zone scores. Increasing the accuracy of documents' relevance ranking is about 4.5% compared to using the weighted average operator. Further, it is assumed to investigate the application of proposed method for determining the weights on the various collections of documents as well as to investigate the practical applicability of the fuzzy integral and fuzzy measure in other tasks of information retrieval such as automatic error correction, automatic abstracting and video annotating.

ACKNOWLEGMENTS

This work was supported by the Ministry of Education and Science of the Russian Federation R & D State project №2.5048.2017 / BP.

REFERENCES

[1]   Beliakov, G., Sola, H. B., & Sánchez, T. C. (2015). *A practical guide to averaging functions* (Vol. 329). Springer.

[2]   Dujmović, J. (2013). Aggregation operators and observable properties of human reasoning. In *Aggregation Functions in Theory and in Practice* (pp. 5-16). Springer Berlin Heidelberg.

[3]   Grabisch, M., Marichal, J. L., Mesiar, R., & Pap, E. *Aggregation Functions.* (2009). Cambridge Univ., Press, Cambridge, UK.

[4]   Choquet, G. (1953). Theory of capacities. In *Annales de l'institut Fourier* (Vol. 5, pp. 131-295).

[5]   Zadeh, L. A. (1965). *Fuzzy sets. Information and control*, 8(3), 338-353.

[6]   Sugeno, M. (1975). *Theory of Fuzzy Integrals and Its Applications.*

[7]   Grabisch, M., Orlovski, S. A., & Yager, R. R. (1998). Fuzzy aggregation of numerical preferences. In *Fuzzy sets in decision analysis, operations research and statistics* (pp. 31-68). Springer US.

[8] Detyniecki, M., Bouchon-meunier, D. B., Yager, D. R., & Prade, R. H. (2000). *Mathematical aggregation operators and their application to video querying.*

[9] Torra, V., & Narukawa, Y. (2007). *Modeling decisions: information fusion and aggregation operators.* Springer Science & Business Media.

[10] Alfimtsev, A., Sakulin, S., & Devyatkov, V. (2012). Web Personalization Based on Fuzzy Aggregation and Recognition of User Activity. *International journal of Web portals* (IJWP), 4(1), 33-41.

[11] Alfimtsev, A., Sakulin, S., & Levanov, A. (2016). Formalization of Expert Knowledge about the Usability of Web Pages Based on User Criteria Aggregation. *International Journal of Software Innovation* (IJSI), 4(3), 38-50.

[12] Sakulin, S., Alfimtsev, A. (2015). The Extension of Weight Determining Method for Weighted Zone Scoring in Information Retrieval. *Journal of Pattern Recognition and Intelligent Systems,* 3(3), 29-35.

[13] Merad, M., Dechy, N., Serir, L., Grabisch, M., & Marcel, F. (2013). Using a multi-criteria decision aid methodology to implement sustainable development principles within an organization. *European Journal of Operational Research,* 224(3), 603-613.

[14] Shapley, L. S. (1953). A value for n-person games. *Contributions to the Theory of Games,* 2(28), 307-317.

[15] Murofushi, T. (1992, October). A technique for reading fuzzy measures (I): the Shapley value with respect to a fuzzy measure. *In 2nd fuzzy workshop* (Vol. 1, No. 1, pp. 39-48).

[16] Murofushi, T., & Soneda, S. (1993, May). Techniques for reading fuzzy measures (III): interaction index. In *9th fuzzy system symposium* (pp. 693-696).

[17] Marichal, J. L. (2000). An axiomatic approach of the discrete Choquet integral as a tool to aggregate interacting criteria. *IEEE Transactions on Fuzzy Systems,* 8(6), 800-807.

[18] Moulin, H. (1991). *Axioms of cooperative decision making* (No. 15). Cambridge University Press.

[19] Fishburn, P. C. (1970). *Utility theory for decision making* (No. RAC-R-105). Research Analysis Corp Mclean va.

[20] Grabisch, M. (1996). The application of fuzzy integrals in multicriteria decision making. *European journal of operational research,* 89(3), 445-456.

[21] Grabisch, M. (1997). K-order additive discrete fuzzy measures and their representation. *Fuzzy sets and systems*, 92(2), 167-189.

[22] Mayag, B., Grabisch, M., & Labreuche, C. (2011). A representation of preferences by the Choquet integral with respect to a 2-additive capacity. *Theory and Decision*, 71(3), 297-324.

[23] Grabisch, M. (2000). A graphical interpretation of the Choquet integral. *IEEE Transactions on Fuzzy Systems*, 8(5), 627-631.

[24] Takahagi, E. (2008). A fuzzy measure identification method by diamond pairwise comparisons and transformation. *Fuzzy Optimization and Decision Making*, 7(3), 219-232.

[25] Wu, J. Z., & Zhang, Q. (2010). 2-order additive fuzzy measure identification method based on diamond pairwise comparison and maximum entropy principle. *Fuzzy Optimization and Decision Making*, 9(4), 435-453.

[26] Sakulin S, Devyatkov V. (2012) Analiz sostoyaniya tekhnologicheskikh protsessov na osnove nechetkikh ekspertnykh znaniy Saarbrucken: Lambert Academic Publishing. [Sakulin S, Devyatkov V. (2012) *Analysis of the technological processes state based on fuzzy expert knowledge* (In Russian). Saarbrucken: Lambert Academic Publishing.]

[27] Grabisch, M., Kojadinovic, I., & Meyer, P. (2008). A review of methods for capacity identification in Choquet integral based multi-attribute utility theory: *Applications of the Kappalab R package. European journal of operational research*, 186(2), 766-785.

[28] Marichal, J. L., & Roubens, M. (2000). Determination of weights of interacting criteria from a reference set. *European journal of operational Research,* 124(3), 641-650.

[29] Kojadinovic, I. (2007). Minimum variance capacity identification. *European Journal of Operational Research*, 177(1), 498-514.

[30] Marichal, J. L. (2002). Entropy of discrete Choquet capacities. *European Journal of Operational Research*, 137(3), 612-624.

[31] Jaynes, E. T. (1957). Information theory and statistical mechanics. *Physical review*, 106(4), 620-630.

[32] Sicilia, M. Á., Barriocanal, E. G., & Calvo, T. (2003). An inquiry-based method for Choquet integral-based aggregation of interface usability parameters. *Kybernetika,* 39(5), 601-614.

[33] Akasaka, Y., & Onisawa, T. (2008). Personalized pedestrian navigation system with subjective preference based route selection. In *Intelligent Decision and Policy Making Support Systems* (pp. 73-91). Springer Berlin Heidelberg.

[34] Jullien, S., Mauris, G., Valet, L., Bolon, P., & Teyssier, S. (2008). Identification of choquet integral's parameters based on relative entropy and applied to classification of tomographic images. In *IPMU* (Vol. 8, pp. 1360-1367).

[35] Martínez, G. E., Mendoza, D. O., Castro, J. R., Melin, P., & Castillo, O. (2017). Choquet Integral and Interval Type-2 Fuzzy Choquet Integral for Edge Detection. In *Nature-Inspired Design of Hybrid Intelligent Systems* (pp. 79-97). Springer International Publishing.

[36] Alfimtsev, A. N., Sakulin, S. A., & Devyatkov, V. V. (2011). Uluchsheniye tsifrovogo izobrazheniya s ispol'zovaniyem nechetkogo operatora Shoke. Vestnik MGTU im. NE Baumana. Ser. Priborostroyeniye. Spets. Vypusk «Informatsionnyye tekhnologiii komp'yuternyye sistemy, 5-12. [Alfimtsev A, Sakulin S, Devyatkov V. Digital image improvement with use of the Choquet fuzzy operator (In Russian). *MSTU Transactions.* 2011; Vol. 1: pages 5-12.]

[37] Liu, H., Wang, X., & Kadir, A. (2013). Color image encryption using Choquet fuzzy integral and hyper chaotic system. *Optik-International Journal for Light and Electron Optics,* 124(18), 3527-3533.

[38] Anderson, M. F., Anderson, D. T., & Wescott, D. J. (2010). *Estimation of adult skeletal age- at- death using the Sugeno fuzzy integral. American journal of physical anthropology*, 142(1), 30-41.

[39] Wu, S. L., Liu, Y. T., Hsieh, T. Y., Lin, Y. Y., Chen, C. Y., Chuang, C. H., & Lin, C. T. (2017). Fuzzy Integral with Particle Swarm Optimization for a Motor-Imagery-Based Brain–Computer Interface. *IEEE Transactions on Fuzzy Systems*, 25(1), 21-28.

[40] Yildiz, A., & Yayla, A. (2017). Application of fuzzy TOPSIS and generalized Choquet integral methods to select the best supplier. *Decision Science Letters*, 6(2), 137-150.

[41] Ameur, S. T. B., Cloppet, F., Dorra, S., & Wendling, L. (2016, February). Choquet Integral based Feature Selection for Early Breast Cancer Diagnosis from MRIs. In *ICPRAM* (pp. 351-358).

[42] Martín, P., Czycholl, I., Buxadé, C., & Krieter, J. (2017). Validation of a multi-criteria evaluation model for animal welfare. *Animal*, 11(4), 650-660.

[43] Xu, K., & Gong, H. (2016). Emergency logistics support capability evaluation model based on triangular fuzzy entropy and Choquet integral. *Journal of Industrial and Production Engineering*, 33(7), 435-442.

[44] Bush, V. (1945). As we may think. *The Atlantic monthly*, 176(1), 101-108.

[45] Sullivan, D. (2009). Google Now Personalizes Everyone's Search Results. *Search Engine Land*, 12.

[46] Gao, M., Liu, K., & Wu, Z. (2010). Personalisation in web computing and informatics: Theories, techniques, applications, and future research. *Information Systems Frontiers*, 12(5), 607-629.

[47] Markellou, P., Rigou, M., & Sirmakessis, S. (2009). Web Personalization for E-Marketing Intelligence. In Human Computer Interaction: *Concepts, Methodologies, Tools, and Applications* (pp. 2164-2180). IGI Global.

[48] Yee, G., & Korba, L. (2010). Security Personalization for Internet and Web Services. In Web Services Research for Emerging Applications: *Discoveries and Trends* (pp. 205-229). IGI Global.

[49] Casas, R., Blasco Marín, R., Robinet, A., Delgado, A., Yarza, A., Mcginn, J., & Grout, V. (2008). User modelling in ambient intelligence for elderly and disabled people. *Computers Helping People with Special Needs*, 114-122.

[50] LeRouge, C., Ma, J., Sneha, S., & Tolle, K. (2013). User profiles and personas in the design and development of consumer health technologies. *International journal of medical informatics*, 82(11), e251-e268.

[51] Verma, V., Verma, A. K., & Bhatia, S. S. (2011). Comprehensive survey of framework for web personalization using web mining. *International Journal of Computer Applications*, 35(3), 23-28.

[52] Salonen, V., & Karjaluoto, H. (2016). Web personalization: The state of the art and future avenues for research and practice. *Telematics and Informatics*, 33(4), 1088-1104.

[53] McIlwraith, D. G., Babenko, D., & Marmanis, H. (2016). *Allgorithms of the intelligent web*. Manning Publ.

[54] Loia, V., Nikravesh, M., & Zadeh, L. A. (2004). *Fuzzy logic and the Internet* (Vol. 137). Springer Science & Business Media.

[55] Lu, J., Ruan, D., & Zhang, G. (2007). E-service intelligence: An introduction. In *E-Service Intelligence* (pp. 1-33). Springer Berlin Heidelberg.

[56] Cui, S., & Feng, B. (2005). A fuzzy integral method to merge search engine results on web. *Computational Intelligence and Security*, 731-736.

[57] Barber, N. A. (2013). Investigating the potential influence of the internet as a new socialization agent in context with other traditional socialization agents. *Journal of Marketing Theory and Practice*, 21(2), 179-194.

[58] Fischer, S., Itoh, M., & Inagaki, T. (2015). Prior schemata transfer as an account for assessing the intuitive use of new technology. *Applied ergonomics*, 46, 8-20.

[59] Horiuchi, H., Saiki, S., Matsumoto, S., & Namamura, M. (2015). Virtual Agent as a User Interface for Home Network System. *International Journal of Software Innovation* (IJSI), 3(2), 13-23.

[60] Fernandez, A., Insfran, E., & Abrahão, S. (2011). Usability evaluation methods for the web: A systematic mapping study. *Information and Software Technology*, 53(8), 789-817.

[61] Dubey, S. K., Gulati, A., Rana, A. (2012). Usability Evaluation of Software Systems using Fuzzy Multi-Criteria Approach. *International Journal of Computer Science Issues*, 9 (2), 404-409.

[62] Chiou, W. C., Lin, C. C., & Perng, C. (2010). A strategic framework for website evaluation based on a review of the literature from 1995–2006. *Information & management*, 47(5), 282-290.

[63] Yang, R., & Ouyang, R. (2014). Classification based on Choquet integral. *Journal of Intelligent & Fuzzy Systems*, 27(4), 1693-1702.

[64] Timonin, M. (2013). Robust optimization of the Choquet integral. *Fuzzy sets and systems*, 213, 27-46.

[65] Mentes, S. A., & Turan, A. H. (2012). Assessing the usability of university websites: an empirical study on Namik Kemal University. *Turkish Online Journal of Educational Technology*, 11 (3), 61–69.

[66] Manzoor, M., & Hussain, W. (2012). A web usability evaluation model for higher education providing Universities of Asia. Science, *Technology and Development*, 31 (2), 183–192.

[67] Okene, D. E., & Enukpere, V. E. (2011). Comparative analysis of the usability of academic websites of Delta State Polytechnics. *Journal of Emerging Trends in Engineering and Applied Sciences*, 2 (6), 1042–1046.

[68] Almahamid, S. M., Tweiqat, A. F., & Almanaseer, M. S. (2016). University website quality characteristics and success: lecturers' perspective. *International Journal of Business Information Systems*, 22(1), 41-61.

[69] Albert, W., & Tullis, T. (2013). *Measuring the User Experience, Second Edition: Collecting, Analyzing, and Presenting Usability Metrics* (Interactive Technologies). Burlington, United States: Morgan Kaufmann.

[70] Zaphiris, P., & Ellis, R. D. (2001). Website Usability and Content Accessibility of the top USA Universities. In proceedings of WebNet 2001 - *World Conference on the WWW and Internet*. Orlando, Usa (pp. 1380-1385).

[71] Roya, S., Pattnaika, P. K., Mal, R. (2014). A quantitative approach to evaluate usability of academic websites based on human perception. *Egyptian Informatics Journal*, 15 (3), 159–167.

[72] Thompson, T., Comden, D., Ferguson, S., Burgstahler, S., Moore, E. J. (2013). Seeking Predictors of Web Accessibility in U.S. Higher Education Institutions. *Information Technology and Disabilities E-Journal*, 13 (1), http://itd. athenpro. org/ volume13/ number1/ thompson.html

[73] Manning, C. D., Raghavan, P., & Schütze, H. (2008*). Introduction to information retrieval* (Vol. 1, No. 1, p. 496). Cambridge: Cambridge university press.

[74] Ceri, S., Bozzon, A., Brambilla, M., Della Valle, E., Fraternali, P., & Quarteroni, S. (2013). *Web information retrieval. Springer Science & Business Media.*

[75] Büttcher, S., Clarke, C. L., & Cormack, G. V. (2016). *Information retrieval: Implementing and evaluating search engines*. Mit Press.

[76] Robertson, S., Zaragoza, H., & Taylor, M. (2004, November). Simple BM25 extension to multiple weighted fields. In *Proceedings of the thirteenth ACM international conference on Information and knowledge management* (pp. 42-49). ACM.

[77] Robertson, S. E., & Walker, S. (1994, August). Some simple effective approximations to the 2-poisson model for probabilistic weighted retrieval. In *Proceedings of the 17th annual international ACM SIGIR conference on Research and development in information retrieval* (pp. 232-241). Springer-Verlag New York, Inc.

[78] Cohen, W. W., & Singer, Y. (1999). Context-sensitive learning methods for text categorization. *ACM Transactions on Information Systems (TOIS)*, 17(2), 141-173.

[79] Murata, M., Ma, Q., Uchimoto, K., Ozaku, H., Utiyama, M., & Isahara, H. (2000, November). Japanese probabilistic information

retrieval using location and category information. In *Proceedings of the fifth international workshop on on Information retrieval with Asian languages* (pp. 81-88). ACM.

[80] Svore, K. M., & Burges, C. J. (2009, November). A machine learning approach for improved BM25 retrieval. In *Proceedings of the 18th ACM conference on Information and knowledge management* (pp. 1811-1814). ACM.

[81] Tehrani, A. F., Cheng, W., & Hullermeier, E. (2012). Preference learning using the choquet integral: The case of multipartite ranking. *IEEE Transactions on Fuzzy Systems,* 20(6), 1102-1113.

[82] Hüllermeier, E., & Tehrani, A. F. (2013). Efficient learning of classifiers based on the 2-additive Choquet integral. *In Computational Intelligence in Intelligent Data Analysis* (pp. 17-29). Springer Berlin Heidelberg.

[83] Wu, J., Yang, S., Zhang, Q., & Ding, S. (2015). 2-Additive Capacity Identification Methods from Multicriteria Correlation Preference Information. *IEEE Transactions on Fuzzy Systems*, 23(6), 2094-2106.

ABOUT THE AUTHORS

Sergey A. Sakulin graduated the Bauman Moscow State Technical University in 2001. He is a PhD by BMSTU in 2009. Today he is an assistant professor of Information systems and telecommunications department. He has 26 scientific papers. Scientific interests lie in the fields of artificial intelligence methods and expert knowledge formalization and visualization.

Email: sakulin@bmstu.ru.

Alexander N. Alfimtsev graduated the Bauman Moscow State Technical University in 2005, PhD by BMSTU in 2008. He is an associated professor at BMSTU, Information systems and telecommunications department. He has 70 scientific papers, including three patents for inventions. Scientific interests lie in the fields of intelligent multimodal interfaces, machine learning and computer vision.

Email: alfim@bmstu.ru, RG:

https://www.researchgate.net/profile/Alexander_Alfimtsev.

In: Data Fusion
Editors: V. Albert and E. Aba

ISBN: 978-1-53612-720-1
© 2017 Nova Science Publishers, Inc.

Chapter 2

DATA FUSION APPLIED TO FOOD ANALYSIS

Bruno G. Botelho[1] and Adriana S. Franca[2],*
[1]DQ [2]DEMEC, Universidade Federal de Minas Gerais
Belo Horizonte, MG, Brasil

ABSTRACT

In recent years, the application of chemometric methods in food analysis has gained great importance. It allows for fast, simple and, most of the time, non-destructive determination of micro and macro constituents, physical and chemical properties, and detection of adulteration, among other possibilities. Foodstuffs are known for being highly complex matrices, and one single analytical technique may, sometimes, not provide all the necessary information for the required method. A natural step for the development of methods for this type of matrix is to combine two or more techniques, in order to increase the range of information about the samples and exploit the possibility of merging information from different sources. This data fusion can lead to a more accurate knowledge about the samples and also provide methods

---

* Corresponding Author Email: adriana@demec.ufmg.br.; Tel: +55-31-34093512. Fax: +55-31-34433783.

with improved prediction capacity. In this review, the concept of data fusion, its fundaments and its application in different areas of food analysis will be explored.

1. INTRODUCTION

The assessment of food quality is a multifaceted task, which involves the estimation of its composition, properties, flavors and the control of changes that occur during the stages of the industrial processing. Measuring quality, safety, sensory and nutritional properties and stability are the main concerns of food scientists working on the industry or in academic or governmental laboratories (McGorrin 2009).

In the beginning of the 20th century, all the food analysis methods were based in "wet chemistry", which consists of simple analytical procedures, using simple equipment (glassware, weighing balances, ovens, and Bunsen burners among others) combined with complex and sequential procedures (mixing, filtering, solvent extraction, drying, weighing, evaporation, distillation, etc.). The foundations of the methods used in the early days of food analysis were derived from chemical methods of isolation and analysis of organic substances that have been developed since the beginning of the 1800s. Some of the methods established in the wet chemistry era of food analysis continue to be used as reference methods in different areas until today. Fat, moisture and protein determinations in a great range of food products are still determined the same way as it was done 100 years ago (McGorrin 2009; Cifuentes 2012).

An alternative to overcome the disadvantages of the traditional food analysis methods cited so far was the use of instrumental analysis jointly with chemometric methods. Karl H. Norris, an employee from the United States Department of Agriculture (USDA) was the pioneer in using Near Infrared Spectroscopy (NIRS) and multivariate statistical treatment for food analysis. He started developing methods for determining moisture in agricultural products by their methanolic extracts (Hart, Norris and

Golumbic 1962), and also published papers showing the application of spectroscopic methods for determining a great variety of properties in different matrixes, such as meat products (Ben-Gera and Norris 1968a), grains and seeds (Delwiche and Norris 1993; Norris and Hart 1996) and milk (Ben-Gera and Norris 1968b). This kind of approach allows the analysis of foodstuff in a very simple, fast and reliable way, with minimal human intervention. Since Karl Norris published his first paper in 1962, a great number of applications have been reported in the literature, using chemometrics in food analysis. The development of methods for the quantification of major and minor components (Rodriguez-Otero, Hermida and Cepeda 1995; Büning-Pfaue 2003; Kim, Singh and Kays 2007; Chitra, Ghosh and Mishra 2016; Ouyang, Chen and Zhao 2016; Peng et al. 2016), physical-chemical properties (Zheng, Sun and Zheng 2006; Mendoza, Dejmek and Aguilera 2007; Kuo and Gunasekaran 2009; Guelpa et al. 2015; Ahmad et al. 2016), antibiotic residues (Ni, Li and Kokot 2011; Zhong, Ni and Kokot 2012; Hernández et al. 2015), additives (Botelho, De Assis and Sena 2014; Qiu and Wang 2017), determination of geographic origin (Longobardi et al. 2015; Gaiad et al. 2016; Marseglia et al. 2016; Karabagias et al. 2017) and detection of frauds and adulteration (Alamprese et al. 2016; Dong et al. 2017; Pasias, Kiriakou and Proestos 2017; Zhu, Wang and Chen 2017) have been reported in the literature coupled to chemometrics.

A natural step in the improvement of chemometric models is to combine information from two or more sources in order to obtain more information about the studied samples. This strategy is called data fusion (DF). DF consists of a group of data integration mechanisms that combine data from different sources in order to improve the quality of the information extracted from them. The concept of data fusion arose in the 1970s, in the military field, for target identification, airborne early warnings, weapon guidance, battlefield surveillance, local defense, command and control. In non-military, it was used in computational methods dedicated to provide medical diagnostics, remote sensing, monitoring and control of large engineering environment and systems and robotics (Pan et al. 1998; Coutto Filho, Souza and Schilling 2007).

The human brain is very efficient in combining data from different sources to make decisions. This is a crucial ability when it comes to better understanding your surroundings and identifying threats (Pan et al. 1998). Our five senses (sight, sound, smell, taste and touch) are combined with previous knowledge of the environment to create and update a dynamic model of the world (Elmenreich 2002). When we taste any food, the senses are combined in order to establish our sensory perception of that product. This capacity of merging multiple senses in one quality statement was the basis for the application of DF in food analysis. It was first applied in the determination of fruit characteristics, such as firmness, maturity and sugar content (Steinmetz et al. 1996, 1997, 1999), juice freshness and type (Wide et al. 1998) and quality of crispbread, a traditional Swedish cracker (Winquist et al. 1999). Since them, the application of data fusion to food analysis has developed from more than just mimicking our senses to analyses using high end techniques, just as chromatography, nuclear magnetic resonance, spectroscopy and others. In this chapter, some basic concepts and some recent applications of data fusion in food analysis will be presented.

2. BASIC ASPECTS OF DATA FUSION

2.1. Definition

Although DF is not a new subject, there is still no consensus about its definition, or even if Data Fusion is the correct name for this field of research. Different terms, such as "sensor fusion", "data fusion", information fusion", multi-sensor data fusion", and multi-sensor integration" can be found in technical literature with similar meanings. All these terms define processes more than the field itself, so each proposed definition may be profound in some aspects and very superficial or even negligent in others (Elmenreich 2002).

After reviewing a great number of definition, Broström et al. (2007) proposed a more complete definition. According to the authors,

"Information Fusion is the study of the efficient methods for automatically or semi-automatically transforming information from different sources and different points in time into a representation that provides effective support for human or automated decision making".

and the terms "data fusion" and "sensor fusion" may be considered special cases of Information Fusion, and in some cases, they may even be considered synonyms (Boström et al. 2007). In food analysis, both "Sensor Fusion" and "Data Fusion" are commonly used, but Sensor Fusion (SF) is more common when the data acquisition is performed through a sensor array, and DF is more used when data comes from traditional instrumental methods.

2.2. Advantages and Limitations of Data Fusion

When multiple information about a sample is obtained, a number of benefits over a single data system are expected. DF systems have an inherent redundancy that enables them to provide correct information even if one of the data sources suffers an unexpected variation, making DF systems more robust and reliable. This redundancy, in some level, also increases the confidence of the system because one sensor may confirm the measurement of the other (e.g., same substance being detected by a near infrared spectrophotometer (NIR) and a mid infrared spectrophotometer (MIR)). If repeated measures of the same nature are done in the same sample (e.g., repeated measurements of the firmness in different points of a peach), a spatial coverage may be achieved, providing a better description of the analyzed sample (Steinmetz et al. 1996; Steinmetz, Sevila and Bellon-Maurel 1999; Elmenreich 2002).

Although presenting a series of advantages, DF also has its drawbacks. It is important to remember that each new source of information that is added to a system results in more costs (acquisition, operation and maintenance) and more time for processing the data, and this increase may not reflect in any improvement in the results. Moreover, it must be considered if each newly added information will contribute with relevant information to the model. Excess of information may sometimes lower the capacity of a model in providing correct answers, depending on the fusion architectures used (Nahin and Pokoski 1980; Dasarathy 2000). Fowler (1979) analyzed the relations between cost and performance in military systems, in which he highlighted that high investments may not always result in significant improvements, and one of the criticized point is the overestimation of data fusion capacity.

"Be wary of proposals of synergistic systems. Most of time when you try to make 2 + 2 = 5, you end up with 3…and sometimes 1.9". (Fowler 1979; Nahin and Pokoski 1980).

2.3. Three- Level Characterization

Data Fusion techniques may be divided into three different levels, depending on how the data in fused. These levels are called low, intermediate and high level. In low-level data fusion (LLDF), also called raw data fusion, the signals from different sources are combined without any processing (Figure 1).

Because low level is based on raw data, it is necessary that these signals have some similarity, such as two images from the same sample, or absorptions in different wavelength ranges (Steinmetz, Sevila and Bellon-Maurel 1999; Elmenreich 2002; Borràs et al. 2015; Geurts et al. 2015). Data generated from correlation spectroscopy may also be considered LLDF. In this approach, the outputs from two different instruments are multiplied, resulting in a three-dimensional matrix that represents all the possible relations between them. This matrix can be analyzed by three way methods, like PARAFAC (Pararell Factor Analysis), NPLS (N-way Partial

Least Squares) or MCR (Multivariate Curve Resolution) (Yang et al. 2015).

The main advantage of LLDF is the simplicity, because it is only necessary to concatenate all the data in one single matrix. It uses one single model and can highlight correlations between data from different sources. On the other hand, the amount of data used in LLDF may become too large if a high number of sensors is used; the possible dominance of one data source over the others may also be a problem. This can be partially overcome using intermediate level data fusion (ILDF) (Borràs et al. 2015; Geurts et al. 2015).

Reis et al. (2017) used LLDF to propose a screening method for the simultaneous detection of four adulterants (spent coffee grounds, roasted coffee husks, roasted corn and roasted barley) in roasted and ground coffee. MIR spectra of the coffee samples adulterated with up to four adulterants were acquired by two different sampling techniques: Attenuated Total Reflectance (ATR) and Diffuse Reflectance (DRIFTS) and the data were fused in order to verify if they could be used to discriminate pure from adulterated coffee samples using PLS-DA (Partial Least Squares Discriminant Analysis). When compared to the models built with individual acquisition modes, LLDF clearly improved model performance, reducing the number of misclassified samples in the test set from around 14.5% (ATR model) and 14.7% (DRIFTS model) down to 4.5% after DF (Reis et al. 2017).

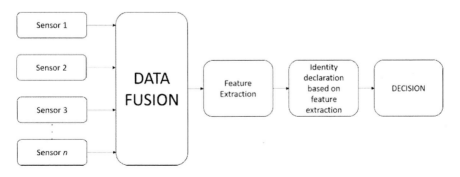

Figure 1. Low-level data fusion (LLDF).
(Adapted from Steinmetz, Sevila and Bellon-Maurel 1999).

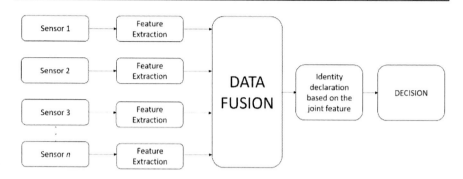

Figure 2. Intermediate Level Data Fusion (ILDF).
(Adapted from Steinmetz, Sevila and Bellon-Maurel 1999).

ILDF, also called mid level data fusion or feature level data fusion, is based on the extraction of features (relevant information) from the data generated by each sensor prior to the fusion (Figure 2) (Steinmetz, Sevila and Bellon-Maurel 1999). Usually the scores from a PCA (Principal Component Analysis) or a PLS-DA are used, but any other informative vector, such as the VIP Scores (Variable Importance Projection Scores), regression coefficient or the NAS (Net Analyte Signal) or variable selection methods may be used. ILDF will significantly reduce the data volume and allow each information block to be treated individually, which improves the model interpretability. The challenge in ILDF is to achieve the optimal combination of extracted features and pre-processing that provides the best model (Geurts et al. 2015).

Silvestri et al. (2014) fused data from H^1 Nuclear Magnetic Ressonance (H-NMR), Excitation-Emission Matrix Fluorescence (EEM) and High Pressure Liquid Chromatography coupled with Diode Array Detection (HPLC-DAD) for varietal classification of Lambrusco PDO wines (Grasparossa, Salamino or Sorbara). Given that the data used presented different dimensions (EEM is three-dimensional while H-NMR and HPLC-DAD are bidimensional), ILDF was used. H-NMR features were extracted using PCA, PARAFAC was used to extract the features from EEM and MCR was used in the chromatographic data. All the extracted features were fused and a PCA was performed (Silvestri et al. 2014).

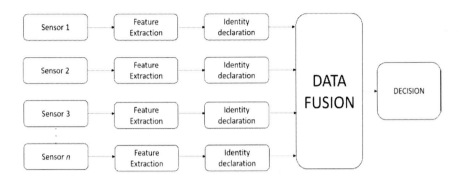

Figure 3. High Level Data Fusion (HLDF).
(Adapted from Steinmetz, Sevila and Bellon-Maurel 1999).

High Level Data Fusion (HLDF), also called Decision Level, is based on the fusion of the identity provided by the different information sources (Figure 3). A classification or regression model is built for each source, and an identity declaration (e.g., a quality class classification) is obtained for each data source. The identity declarations from all sources are then fused using heuristic techniques, Bayesian techniques, Dempster-Shafer methods or Generalized Evidence Processing (GEP) (Steinmetz et al. 1999; Roussel et al. 2003; Borràs et al. 2015; Geurts et al. 2015). The main advantage of HLDF over the other levels is that data from each source are treated and modelled separately, which allows for better extraction of the relevant information. HLDT also is more robust with respect to non-relevant data, so results from inefficient sources do not worsen the performance in the same way they would in LLDF and ILDF (Roussel et al. 2003; Borràs et al. 2015; Geurts et al. 2015).

Rousell et al. (2003) used HLDF in order to classify different varieties of white grapes. An array of aroma sensors, mid infrared spectra and UV/VIS spectra were used to build separate classification models using PLS-DA models. Each sample could be classified in four different classes: "Sauvignon", "Mauzac", "Colombard" and "Others". The classifications of each PLS-DA model were fused using the Bayesian Minimum risk classification rule. The application of HLDF reduced the classification errors from 9.6%, in the mid infrared model (individual model with the smallest error) to 4.7% (Roussel et al. 2003).

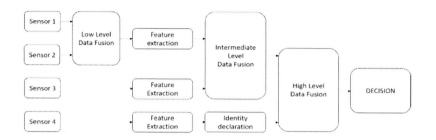

Figure 4. Hybrid level schematic representation.
(Adapted from Steinmetz, Sevila and Bellon-Maurel 1999).

It is also possible to combine different levels of DF in the same application, creating "hybrid" data fusion systems (Borràs et al. 2015). Consider as an example an array of four sensor, where data from sensor 1 and 2 are fused at low level. The feature extracted from the LLDF is fused at intermediate level with feature information extracted from sensor 3, and an identity declaration is stated. This declaration in then fused at high level with the identity declaration from sensor 4, and the final decision from the hybrid model is obtained (Figure 4).

In theory, the most efficient way to fuse data is through LLDF, because it uses all the information provided by the equipment, but some practical aspects must be considered. When all data is used, non-relevant information and noise are present, and this could decrease the model performance. LLDF usually also demands high memory capacity and high-speed data processing. ILDF and HLDF, on the other hand, are less affected by noise and non-relevant information, because the features are extracted and used in the model construction. They also demand less processing capacity and memory capacity. However, if the features extraction is not done properly, the models may not perform as well as expected (Steinmetz et al. 1999; Geurts et al. 2015).

3. APPLICATIONS

The assessment of quality in food analysis, most of the time, is not related to one single parameter. When the focus is on sensory quality, physical properties, such as firmness, crunchiness, texture, viscosity and color, and chemical properties, such as acidity, pH, phenolic compounds, sugar, water, lipid and protein content play different and simultaneous roles in the definition of a "good" or "suitable" product for a specific application. Other applications, such as geographical origin determination or adulteration detection are based more in fingerprinting than quantifying specific compounds. Moreover, it is very unlikely that one single equipment or analytical technique is capable of providing reliable information for all of these applications (Steinmetz, Sevila and Bellon-Maurel 1999).

The alternative proposed by some food scientists was to try to mimic the human brain capacity of simultaneously acquiring and combining sensory data in order to define an opinion about a sample. The first applications of DF in food analysis were mainly based on sensors that tried to simulate human senses like vision, smell, touch and taste (Steinmetz, Sevila and Bellon-Maurel 1999).

3.1. The Early Days: Data Fusion from Sensor Analysis Applied to Control of Fruits and Vegetables

The utilization of modern instrumental analysis in food analysis began only in the 1980s, with the advent of the semiconductor technology, computing technology and the laser. It truly consolidated only at the end of the century (McGorrin 2009), so, before that, the alternative to perform complex measures in foodstuffs was the application of sensors. It was a smart alternative, capable of generating a series of information about the samples in a simple, and, most of the time, nondestructive way. Sensors were applied in the measurement of all kinds of foods, but they were remarkably important for the analysis of fruits (Chen and Sun 1991). A few applications can be seen on Table 1.

Nevertheless, even this strategy was not able to deal with complex measures, such as ripeness and visual appearance of the fruits in every situation. Ripeness is related to overall maturity and can be evaluated according to weight, length, diameter, firmness, color, total soluble solids, acidity, and aroma.

Table 1. Sensor application to fruits analysis

Sensor Type	Product	Measured Property	Reference
Force deformation	Pears	Maturity index detection	(J. J. Mehlschau et al. 1981)
Impact force	Peaches and pears	Classification in three categories of firmness: Hard, firm and soft	(Delwiche, Tang and Mehlschau 1989)
Impact-rebound	Oranges	Separation between damaged and undamaged samples	(Bryan, Barry and Miller 1978)
Sonic Vibration	Apples	Fruit size and firmness	(Abbott et al. 1968)
Acoustic Response	Apples and watermelons	Firmness and sensory measurements	(Yamamoto, Iwamoto and Haginuma 1980, 1981)
Ultrasonic methods	Apples	Bruises detection	(Upchurch et al. 1987)
Computer Vision System	Apples	Detection of watercore	(Throop, Rehkugler and Upchurch 1989)

Visual appearance can be accessed by the evaluation of color, size uniformity, netting, presence and extent of bruises. The combination of these parameters directly affects the fruit quality, and requires more than one information to correctly classify the samples (Dull 1986). Therefore, combining two or more sensors trough DF was the alternative to deal with such a complex task. Information from different sensors, measuring different properties, when fused, could provide useful information about the samples (Ozer, Engel and Simon 1995). Freshness, firmness, color, and other parameters were measured using physical, visual and electronic sensors, and then fused, aiming to classify morphological, physiological and sensory attributes of the products. Quinn et al. (1995) developed an electronic nose named "fruit sniffer", which was composed of a series of chemical sensors (limonene, ethanol, humidity and temperature sensors) capable of classifying citrus fruits in accordance with their ripening stage ("good", "borderline" and "bad"). The sensors were housed in a handheld car vacuum cleaner, to make the system portable (Quinn, Yaxley and

Knight 1995). In another application, an electronic nose composed of four sensors (two sensors detecting volatile organic compounds, one detecting hydrocarbons and volatile gases and the last one detecting carbon monoxide) were also applied successfully to determine the ripeness level of bananas. The authors used the headspace from a vessel containing the samples, and compared to a "blank" headspace, obtained from an empty reference vessel (Figure 5). The signals obtained from the sample vessel were corrected using the reference vessel signals, and then were fused and treated using PCA, self-organizing map (SOM) and Fuzzy-Cluster analysis (Llobet et al. 1999).

Steinmetz et al. (1996) used HLDF to combine information from three different sensors to classify peaches. An impact-response based sensor, which provided as information fruit firmness data; a sound based sensor, which is capable of indicating the resonance frequency of the fruit that can be related to its stiffness; and a micro deformation sensor, which also provides information about the fruit firmness. A representation of the micro deformation sensor can be seen on Figure 6. Destructive methods for the determination of the peaches stiffness and firmness were also performed as reference methods. The HLDF model presented an error rate of 14%, which was smaller than any of the models based on individual sensors, that presented errors rate ranging from 19 to 28% (Steinmetz et al. 1996). Others applications of DF on sensor data are shown on Table 2.

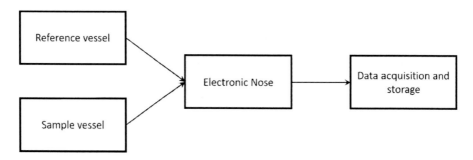

Figure 5. Experimental set-up for the analysis of the banana headspace using an electronic nose.
(Adapted from Llobet et al. 1999).

Table 2. Data fusion applied to fruit analysis

Product	Techniques fused	Data Fusion Level	Reference Parameters	Objective	Ref.
Orange	Computer Vision System Impact Sensor Near Infrared Spectroscopy	Low	Sugar content Acidity Visual classification	To predict maturity and sensory characteristics	(Steinmetz et al. 1997)
Apple	Computer Vision System Near Infrared Spectroscopy	Intermediate	Sugar Content	To quantify sugar content using nondestructive techniques	(Steinmetz et al. 1999)
Juices	Electronic Tongue Electronic Nose	High	Sensory analysis	To identify juice type and freshness	(Wide et al. 1998)
Melons	Computer Vision Electronic Nose Near Infrared	Intermediate	Sugar content Firmness	To determine sugar content and firmness	(Steinmetz et al. 1995)
Tomato es	Computer Vision Drop impact sensor Resonance Frequency sensor Cyclic deformation	Intermediate	Firmness	To classify according to maturity stage	(Edan et al. 1997)
Wheat	Computer Vision	High	Granular parameters of milled wheat	To determine granular parameters of milled wheat	(Ros, Guillaume and Bellon-Maurel 1997)

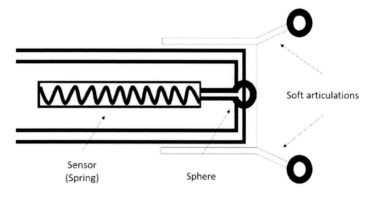

Figure 6. A micro deformation sensor
(Adapted from (Steinmetz et al. 1996).

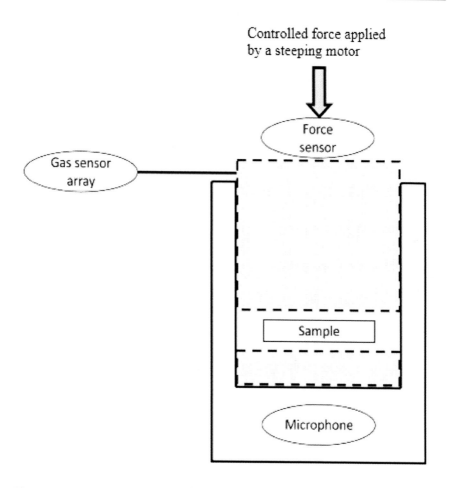

Figure 7. Crush Chamber used for simultaneous analysis of three sensors.
(Adapted from Winquist et al. 1999).

Data obtained from a set of sensors were also used for other types of
foodstuff. Winquist et al. (1999) built a "Crush Chamber", in which they
could crush crispbread, a traditional Swedish cracker, under controlled
conditions. This chamber was equipped with different sensors (Figure 7),
mimicking the human hearing (a microphone), touch (force sensor) and
smell (an electronic nose with 14 sensors). Some features were extracted
from the audio data (position of peaks, size of peaks, kurtosis, mean and
standard deviation), from tactile data (coefficients in a polynomial fit,

kurtosis, mean and standard deviation), and data from electronic nose was used "as is", resulting in a hybrid LLDF-ILDF model. Data were analyzed using PCA and Artificial Neural Networks (ANN). Using the fused data, the authors were able to discriminate crispbread from different brands (Winquist et al. 1999).

Schweizer-Berberich et al. (1994) used an array of 8 gas sensors to estimate fish freshness. Four of the sensors were for CO measuring, two for H_2S, one for SO_2 and one for NO. These sensors were exposed to headspace gases from a polyethylene pouch containing a trout piece, stored for 26 days at 3 °C. Once a day, the headspace from the pouch containing the volatile products was pumped in the direction of the sensors. A heating filament adjusted the gas temperature to seven different levels: 30, 100, 200, 500, 600, 750 and 900°C. By using this strategy, the authors were able to identify and quantify 19 compounds (methanol, ethanol, 1-propanol, 1-butanol, 1-pentanol, 1-hexanol, 1-octanol, 2-butanol, acetone, 2-butanone, ammonia, trimethylamine, hydrogen sulfide, dimethylsulfide, 1-penten-3-ol, 2-hexenal, 1-octen-3-ol, 2-octenal and 2,6-nonadienal). PCA was employed in order to relate concentration and storage time, and the authors were also capable of predicting the concentration of sulfur and nitrogen with low uncertainty, in concentrations ranging from 20 – 300 vpm using Principal Component Regression (PCR) (Schweizer-Berberich, Vaihinger and Göpel 1994).

Fusion of sensor data continues to be largely applied to analysis of fruits and vegetables (Li, Heinemann and Sherry 2007; Chatterjee, Bhattacharjee and Bhattacharyya 2014; Hong and Wang 2014; Hong, Wang and Qiu 2014; Wang and Li 2015; Pourkhak et al. 2017), but its applications have expanded to others matrices, such as beer (Ghasemi-Varnamkhasti et al. 2012; Kutyła-Olesiuk et al. 2012; Gutiérrez et al. 2013), rice wine (Ouyang, Zhao and Chen 2014), tea (Huo et al. 2014; Li et al. 2017), dairy products (Cimander, Carlsson and Mandenius 2002; Henningsson et al. 2006), eggs (Yongwei et al. 2009), sea products (Amari et al. 2006; Limbo et al. 2009; Zhang et al. 2009) and meat (Rajamäki et al. 2006; Balasubramanian et al. 2008; Ghasemi-Varnamkhasti et al. 2009), among others.

3.2. Current Trends in Data Fusion – Food Authentication

The concept of food authentication can be defined as the analytical process capable of providing information about the origin or production process of a food product, and it has gained a lot of attention recently, mainly due two of its aspects: identification of geographical origin and detection of frauds and adulterations (Luykx and van Ruth 2008; Drivelos et al. 2014; Danezis et al. 2016a, 2016b)

Historically, the environment, resources availability and the known food processing technology always influenced dietary habits of a population. Nevertheless, with globalization and the growth of the food industry, a massification of the eating habits has occurred. In recent years, however, consumers began to pay more attention to food origin and its history. The association between a specific producing region with health benefits, patriotism or lack of confidence in foreign products, or the concern about safe and environmentally friend productive process have gained importance in the consumer decisions (Luykx and van Ruth 2008; Drivelos et al. 2014; Danezis et al. 2016b).

The adulteration or fraud in foodstuff is known since immemorial times, and consists in accidentally or deliberately adding chemical or physical substances that should not be present for legal or other reasons (Reis, Franca and Oliveira 2013a, 2013b). The detection of frauds and adulterations has drawn a lot of attention over the past decade due to several scandals. The act of altering a food product composition is not only important from the economical point of view. Some adulterations pose serious threats to the consumers health, such as the milk scandals in China (Gossner et al. 2009) and Brazil (Botelho et al. 2015), the addition of lead salts to spices to enhance their color, and the use of formalin to make fish look fresher (Lohumi et al. 2015; Sørensen, Khakimov and Engelsen 2016).

Foodstuffs are very complex matrices, and the complexity of quality determination related to them is thus also complex, because it is usually not only dependent of a great number of very different substances, but also on their interaction. Therefore, it is very unlikely that one single measurement could provide all necessary information needed. The application of DF to food authentication has gained a lot of attention because it allows the gathering of information from different analytical sources about a same sample, which provides a better interpretation of its components, providing more accurate information about the samples and yielding better inferences (Borràs et al. 2015).

3.2.1. Wine and Beer

Recent researches have shown that the origin of a wine is the most relevant attribute in the consumers purchase process, being sometimes more important than the wine price, so the development of analytical methods capable of differentiating wines according to origin has increased significantly (Schlesier et al. 2009; García-Gallego, Chamorro-Mera and García-Galán 2015).

Cozzolino et al. (2011) proposed a LLDF method using UV/VIS, NIR and MIR to classify *Sauvignon Blanc* wines from different geographical origins (Australia and New Zealand). Data were evaluated using PCA, PLS-DA and Soft Independent Modelling of Class Analogy (SIMCA). According to the authors, the best results were obtained combining NIR and MIR data in a PLS-DA model, with 93% of correct classification for both classes (Cozzolino et al. 2011). Magnetic Nuclear Resonance (NMR) and Site-Specific Natural Isotope Fractionation – Nuclear Magnetic Resonance (SNIF-NMR) were also successfully fused at intermediate level in order to classify German wines according to their geographical origin, vintage year and grape variety (Monakhova et al. 2014). Glycerol, ethanol, °Brix, malic and o-cumaric acids concentrations, anthocyanin and total polyphenols content of wines were determined using MIR and UV/VIS spectra and DF was employed for model development (Sen et al. 2016). These two last parameters were also determined by the combination of Raman and MIR in Chinese rice wine. According to the authors, models obtained by the combination of the features extracted from data generated by both equipment improved the prediction of total antioxidant capacity measured by three methods (FRAP – Ferric Ion Reducing Antioxidant Power, ABTS and DPPH) and the total phenolic content (Wu et al. 2015).

Figure 8. Authentic Trappist Product Seal.
(International Trappist Association (ITA) 2017).

When it comes to beer consumption, the region of origin is not as relevant as it is to wine. However, a special exception can be highlighted. Trappist beers are a particular group of beers produced exclusively by the Trappist Monks, and these are recognized worldwide for its extremely high quality. In order to be considered a Trappist beer, it has to be produced in one the 20 Trappist monasteries of the Order of The Cistercians of the Strict Observance and also measure up to the traditional standards rooted in the monastic life of the community. In order to strengthen the recognition and prevent non-Trappist companies of using its name, the monks created the International Trappist Association (ITA), and created the denomination of "Authentic Trappist Product" (Figure 8).(International Trappist Association (ITA) 2017)

Due to the necessity of discriminating between Trappist and other beers, the organizers of the "Chemométrie", an annual congress on chemometrics posed a challenge for the participants: to develop a method capable of discriminating a specific brand of Trappist beer (Trappist Rochefort 8°) from other Trappist beers and also from non-Trappist beer. All the samples were measured using three techniques (NIR, MIR and Raman). Three participants accepted the challenge, and the organizers used the classifications from the three participants to build an HLDF model for Trappist beer classification (Fernández Pierna et al. 2012).

Table 3. Region of Origin of olive oil discrimination using DF

Country	Techniques Used	Fusion Level	Reference
Italy	UV/VIS	Low	(Casale et al. 2012)
	NIR		
	MIR		
	Fatty Acid Composition		
Italy	Artificial Nose	Intermediate	(Forina et al. 2015)
	NIR		
	UV/VIS		
Morocco	Electronic nose	Low	(Haddi et al. 2013)
	Electronic tongue		
Italy	Artificial Nose	Intermediate	(Casale et al. 2010)
	NIR		
	UV/VIS		
France	NIR	Low	(Dupuy et al. 2010)
	MID		
Spain	Physical-Chemical descriptor	Low	(Pizarro et al. 2013)
	UV/VIS		
Italy	NIR	Low	(Bevilacqua et al. 2012)
	MIR		

3.2.2. Olive Oil

Olive oil (OO) is recognized worldwide by its health benefits and distinguishable taste. The quality of OO is established by international regulations, and it can be classified as inedible (not suitable for human consumption) or edible (suitable for consumption). However, depending on the type of olives used, physical chemical criteria or sensory analysis, it can be further classified into subclasses that can greatly affect its commercial value (Marx et al. 2017).

The EU has been supporting the differentiation of traditional local products, through an integrated framework for the protection of geographical origin by specific regulation (EU Regulations 2081/1992 and 510/2006). To safeguard consumers from frauds, there must be analytical methods capable of verifying the region of origin of an OO, and also of discriminating it from OO produced in nearby regions or in other countries (Casale et al. 2012). As can be seen on Table 3, DF models with a great variety of techniques have been applied in the discrimination of region of origin of olive oils.

3.2.3. Honey

Honey is, by definition, a viscous, supersaturated sugar solution derived from nectar gathered and modified by honeybees, and in accordance to the various international regulations, the addition of any kind of substance to honey is prohibited, consisting of adulteration. Due to its sensory characteristics and health benefits, there is a high market demand for pure honey. This instigates irresponsible sellers to add variants of sugar to honey in order to increase their profits (Subari et al. 2012).

Subari et al. (2012) intentionally adulterated Malaysian pure honey with cane and beet sugar, in concentrations of 20, 40, 60 and 80%. These samples were analyzed by an electronic nose composed of 32 sensors and by MIR. Supervised classification models (Linear Discrimant Analysis – LDA) were used to discriminate between pure and adulterated honey. Data were evaluated separately and through LLDF and ILDF, and the best results were obtained using the LLDF (correct classification rates higher than 90%) (Subari et al. 2012). Mansan et al. (2012) also used DF to study Malaysian honey. However, they discriminated honeys from different floral origins and producers, using the combination of an electronic nose (32 sensors) and an electronic tongue (7 sensors). LDA was used to build classification model using data separately and fused. In this particular study, data fusion did not improve the model performance. Electronic nose data alone was capable of providing a 100% correct classification, whereas the ILDF model provided a correct classification rate of 98% (Masnan et al. 2012).

More advanced techniques, NMR and two kinds of mass spectrometry (Orbitrap-MS and TOF-MS) were used in the origin identification of floral honeys from four different origins (acacia, orange blossom, lavender and eucalyptus), multifloral honey and mountain honey from different countries. ILDF was used in two different strategies: feature extraction by PCA and by variable selection. In both cases, the ILDF PLS-DA model built for honey classification provided better classification than individual models, being capable of discriminating all classes (Spiteri et al. 2016).

CONCLUSION

The application of data fusion in food analysis is a growing trend. It has been used for almost 50 years, based on physical and chemical sensors, and has recently has been extensively studied due to new developments in both data acquisition and processing capacity. Modern analytical instrumentation enables the generation of data from different sources in a very short time, which can provide a great range of information from different aspects of the same sample. This is especially relevant to food analysis, because of the complexity of the samples.

The application of two or more techniques fused in food analysis is an effective tool for the improvement of complex analysis, but one must be aware that the combination of a large number of techniques may also increase the complexity of analytical procedures. Before merging all techniques available, a previous evaluation must be done to verify if all used equipment can really provide relevant information. As stated by Fowler, the objective of data fusion is to obtain 5 by summing 2 + 2; nevertheless, if an indiscriminate use of techniques is performed without any scientific basis, the result can be 3, or even less.

ACKNOWLEDGMENTS

Prof. A. S. Franca acknowledges financial support from Brazilian Government Agencies CNPq and FAPEMIG.

REFERENCES

Abbott JA, Bachman GS, Childers NF et al. Sonic techniques for measuring texture of fruits and vegetables. *Food Technol* 1968;22:101–12.

Ahmad MH, Nache M, Waffenschmidt S et al. A fluorescence spectroscopic approach to predict analytical, rheological and baking parameters of wheat flours using chemometrics. *J Food Eng* 2016;182:65–71.

Alamprese C, Amigo JM, Casiraghi E et al. Identification and quantification of turkey meat adulteration in fresh, frozen-thawed and cooked minced beef by FT-NIR spectroscopy and chemometrics. *Meat Sci* 2016;121:175–81.

Amari A, El Barbri N, Llobet E et al. Monitoring the Freshness of Moroccan Sardines with a Neural-Network Based Electronic Nose. *Sensors* 2006;6:1209–23.

Balasubramanian S, Panigrahi S, Logue CM et al. Independent component analysis-processed electronic nose data for predicting Salmonella typhimurium populations in contaminated beef. *Food Control* 2008;19:236–46.

Ben-Gera I, Norris KH. Direct Spectrophotometric Determination of Fat and Moisture in Meat Products. *J Food Sci* 1968a;33:64–7.

Ben-Gera I, Norris KH. Influence of fat concentration on the absorption spectrum of milk in the near infrared region. *Isr J Agric Res* 1968b;18:7.

Bevilacqua M, Bucci R, Magrì AD et al. Tracing the origin of extra virgin olive oils by infrared spectroscopy and chemometrics: A case study. *Anal Chim Acta* 2012;717:39–51.

Borràs E, Ferré J, Boqué R et al. Data fusion methodologies for food and beverage authentication and quality assessment – A review. *Anal Chim Acta* 2015;891:1–14.

Boström H, Andler SF, Brohede M et al. On the Definition of Information Fusion as a Field of Research. *IKI Tech Reports* 2007:1–8.

Botelho BG, De Assis LP, Sena MM. Development and analytical validation of a simple multivariate calibration method using digital scanner images for sunset yellow determination in soft beverages. *Food Chem* 2014;159:175–80.

Botelho BG, Reis N, Oliveira LS et al. Development and analytical validation of a screening method for simultaneous detection of five adulterants in raw milk using mid-infrared spectroscopy and PLS-DA. *Food Chem* 2015;181:31–7.

Bryan WL, Barry J, Miller M. Mechanically Assisted Grading of Oranges for Processing. *Trans ASAE* 1978;21:1226–31.

Büning-Pfaue H. Analysis of water in food by near infrared spectroscopy. *Food Chem* 2003;82:107–15.

Casale M, Casolino C, Oliveri P et al. The potential of coupling information using three analytical techniques for identifying the geographical origin of Liguria extra virgin olive oil. *Food Chem* 2010;118:163–70.

Casale M, Oliveri P, Casolino C et al. Characterisation of PDO olive oil Chianti Classico by non-selective (UV-visible, NIR and MIR spectroscopy) and selective (fatty acid composition) analytical techniques. *Anal Chim Acta* 2012;712:56–63.

Chatterjee D, Bhattacharjee P, Bhattacharyya N. Development of methodology for assessment of shelf-life of fried potato wedges using electronic noses: Sensor screening by fuzzy logic analysis. *J Food Eng* 2014;133:23–9.

Chen P, Sun Z. A review of non-destructive methods for quality evaluation and sorting of agricultural products. *J Agric Eng Res* 1991;49:85–98.

Chitra J, Ghosh M, Mishra HN. Rapid quantification of cholesterol in dairy powders using Fourier transform near infrared spectroscopy and chemometrics. *Food Control* 2016;78:342–9.

Cifuentes A. Food Analysis: Present, Future, and Foodomics. *ISRN Anal Chem* 2012;2012:1–16.

Cimander C, Carlsson M, Mandenius CF. Sensor fusion for on-line monitoring of yoghurt fermentation. *J Biotechnol* 2002;99:237–48.

Coutto Filho MB Do, Souza JCS De, Schilling MT. Sobre o problema da integração generalizada de dados. *Sba Control Automação Soc Bras Autom* 2007;18:24–43.

Cozzolino D, Cynkar WU, Shah N et al. Can spectroscopy geographically classify Sauvignon Blanc wines from Australia and New Zealand? *Food Chem* 2011;126:673–8.

Danezis GP, Tsagkaris AS, Brusic V et al. Food authentication: state of the art and prospects. *Curr Opin Food Sci* 2016a;10:22–31.

Danezis GP, Tsagkaris AS, Camin F et al. Food authentication: Techniques, trends & emerging approaches. *TrAC - Trends Anal Chem* 2016b;85:123–32.

Dasarathy B V. More the merrier...or is it? Sensor suite augmentation benefits assessment. *Proc Third Int Conf Inf Fusion* 2000;2:WEC3/20-WEC3/25 vol.2.

Delwiche MJ, Tang S, Mehlschau JJ. *An Impact Force Response Fruit Firmness Sorter.* 1989:321–6.

Delwiche SR, Norris KH. Classification of Hard Red Wheat By Near-Infrared Diffuse Reflectance Spectroscopy. *Cereal Chem* 1993;70:29–35.

Dong W, Zhao J, Hu R et al. Differentiation of Chinese robusta coffees according to species, using a combined electronic nose and tongue, with the aid of chemometrics. *Food Chem* 2017;229:743–51.

Drivelos S a., Higgins K, Kalivas JH et al. Data fusion for food authentication. Combining rare earth elements and trace metals to discriminate "fava Santorinis" from other yellow split peas using chemometric tools. *Food Chem* 2014;165:316–22.

Dull GG. Nondestructive evaluation of quality of stored fruits and vegetables. *Food Technol* 1986;40:106–10.

Dupuy N, Galtier O, Ollivier D et al. Comparison between NIR, MIR, concatenated NIR and MIR analysis and hierarchical PLS model. Application to virgin olive oil analysis. *Anal Chim Acta* 2010;666:23–31.

Edan Y, H. Pasternak, Shmulevich I et al. Color and Firmness classification of fresh market tomatoes. *J Food Sci* 1997;62:793–6.

Elmenreich W. An introduction to sensor fusion. *Austria Vienna Univ Technol* 2002:1–28.

Fernández Pierna JA, Duponchel L, Ruckebusch C et al. Trappist beer identification by vibrational spectroscopy: A chemometric challenge posed at the "Chimiométrie 2010" congress. *Chemom Intell Lab Syst* 2012;113:2–9.

Forina M, Oliveri P, Bagnasco L et al. Artificial nose, NIR and UV-visible spectroscopy for the characterisation of the PDO Chianti Classico olive oil. *Talanta* 2015;144:1070–8.

Fowler CA. Comments on the Cost and Performance of Military Systems. *Aerosp Electron Syst IEEE Trans* 1979;AES-15:2–10.

Gaiad JE, Hidalgo MJ, Villafañe RN et al. Tracing the geographical origin of Argentinean lemon juices based on trace element profiles using advanced chemometric techniques. *Microchem J* 2016;129:243–8.

García-Gallego JM, Chamorro-Mera A, García-Galán M del M. The region-of-origin effect in the purchase of wine:The moderating role of familiarity. *Spanish J Agric Res* 2015;13:1–10.

Geurts BP, Engel J, Rafii B et al. Improving high-dimensional data fusion by exploiting the multivariate advantage. *Chemom Intell Lab Syst* 2015;156:231–40.

Ghasemi-Varnamkhasti M, Mohtasebi SS, Siadat M et al. Meat quality assessment by electronic nose (Machine Olfaction Technology). *Sensors* 2009;9:6058–83.

Ghasemi-Varnamkhasti M, Rodríguez-Méndez ML, Mohtasebi SS et al. Monitoring the aging of beers using a bioelectronic tongue. *Food Control* 2012;25:216–24.

Gossner CME, Schlundt J, Embarek P Ben et al. The melamine incident: Implications for international food and feed safety. *Environ Health Perspect* 2009;117:1803–8.

Guelpa A, Bevilacqua M, Marini F et al. Application of Rapid Visco Analyser (RVA) viscograms and chemometrics for maize hardness characterisation. *Food Chem* 2015;173:1220–7.

Gutiérrez JM, Haddi Z, Amari A et al. Hybrid electronic tongue based on multisensor data fusion for discrimination of beers. *Sensors Actuators B Chem* 2013;177:989–96.

Haddi Z, Alami H, El Bari N et al. Electronic nose and tongue combination for improved classification of Moroccan virgin olive oil profiles. *Food Res Int* 2013;54:1488–98.

Hart JR, Norris KH, Golumbic G. Determination of the moisture content of seeds by near-infrared spectrophotometry of their methanol extracts. *Cereal Chem* 1962;39:94–9.

Henningsson M, Östergren K, Sundberg R et al. Sensor fusion as a tool to monitor dynamic dairy processes. *J Food Eng* 2006;76:154–62.

Hernández KU, Velázquez TG, Revilla GO et al. Development of chemometric models using infrared spectroscopy (MID-FTIR) for detection of sulfathiazole and oxytetracycline residues in honey. *Food Sci Biotechnol* 2015;24:1219–26.

Hong X, Wang J. Detection of adulteration in cherry tomato juices based on electronic nose and tongue: Comparison of different data fusion approaches. *J Food Eng* 2014;126:89–97.

Hong X, Wang J, Qiu S. Authenticating cherry tomato juices-Discussion of different data standardization and fusion approaches based on electronic nose and tongue. *Food Res Int* 2014;60:173–9.

Huo D, Wu Y, Yang M et al. Discrimination of Chinese green tea according to varieties and grade levels using artificial nose and tongue based on colorimetric sensor arrays. *Food Chem* 2014;145:639–45.

International Trappist Association (ITA). Available in < http://www. trappist.be/en/ >

J. J. Mehlschau, P. Chen, L. L. Claypool et al. A Deformeter for Non-Destructive Maturity Detection of Pears. *Trans ASAE* 1981;24:1368–71.

Karabagias IK, Louppis AP, Karabournioti S et al. Characterization and geographical discrimination of commercial Citrus spp. honeys produced in different Mediterranean countries based on minerals, volatile compounds and physicochemical parameters, using chemometrics. *Food Chem* 2017; 217:445–55.

Kim Y, Singh M, Kays SE. Near-infrared spectroscopic analysis of macronutrients and energy in homogenized meals. *Food Chem* 2007;105:1248–55.

Kuo M-I, Gunasekaran S. Effect of freezing and frozen storage on microstructure of Mozzarella and pizza cheeses. *LWT - Food Sci Technol* 2009;42:9–16.

Kutyła-Olesiuk A, Zaborowski M, Prokaryn P et al. Monitoring of beer fermentation based on hybrid electronic tongue. *Bioelectrochemistry* 2012;87:104–13.

Li C, Heinemann P, Sherry R. Neural network and Bayesian network fusion models to fuse electronic nose and surface acoustic wave sensor data for apple defect detection. *Sensors Actuators B Chem* 2007;125:301–10.

Li J, Fu B, Huo D et al. Discrimination of Chinese teas according to major amino acid composition by a colorimetric IDA sensor. *Sensors Actuators B Chem* 2017;240:770–8.

Limbo S, Sinelli N, Torri L et al. Freshness decay and shelf life predictive modelling of European sea bass (Dicentrarchus labrax) applying chemical methods and electronic nose. *LWT - Food Sci Technol* 2009;42:977–84.

Llobet E, Hines EL, Gardner JW et al. Non-destructive banana ripeness determination using a neural network-based electronic nose. *Meas Sci Technol* 1999;10:538–48.

Lohumi S, Lee S, Lee H et al. A review of vibrational spectroscopic techniques for the detection of food authenticity and adulteration. *Trends Food Sci Technol* 2015;46:85–98.

Longobardi F, Casiello G, Ventrella A et al. Electronic nose and isotope ratio mass spectrometry in combination with chemometrics for the characterization of the geographical origin of Italian sweet cherries. *Food Chem* 2015;170:90–6.

Luykx DM a. M, van Ruth S. An overview of analytical methods for determining the geographical origin of food products. *Food Chem* 2008;107:897–911.

Marseglia A, Acquotti D, Consonni R et al. HR MAS 1H NMR and chemometrics as useful tool to assess the geographical origin of cocoa beans - Comparison with HR 1H NMR. *Food Res Int* 2016;85:273–81.

Marx ??tala, Rodrigues N, Dias LG et al. Sensory classification of table olives using an electronic tongue: Analysis of aqueous pastes and brines. *Talanta* 2017;162:98–106.

Masnan MJ, Mahat NI, Zakaria A et al. Enhancing Classification Performance of Multisensory Data through Extraction and Selection of Features. *Procedia Chem* 2012;6:132–40.

McGorrin RJ. One Hundred Years of Progress in Food Analysis. *J Agric Food Chem* 2009;57:8076–88.

Mendoza F, Dejmek P, Aguilera JM. Colour and image texture analysis in classification of commercial potato chips. *Food Res Int* 2007;40:1146–54.

Monakhova YB, Godelmanna R, Hermannc A et al. Synergistic effect of the simultaneous chemometric analysis of 1H NMR spectroscopic and stable isotope (SNIF-NMR,18O, 13C) data: Application to wine analysis Yulia. *Anal Chim Acta* 2014;833:29–39.

Nahin PJ, Pokoski JL. NCTR Plus Sensor Fusion Equals IFFN or Can Two Plus Two Equal Five? *IEEE Trans Aerosp Electron Syst* 1980;AES-16:320–37.

Ni Y, Li S, Kokot S. Simultaneous voltammetric analysis of tetracycline antibiotics in foods. *Food Chem* 2011;124:1157–63.

Norris KH, Hart JR. Direct spectrophotometric determination of moisture content of grain and seeds. *J Near Infrared Spectrosc* 1996;4:23–30.

Ouyang Q, Chen Q, Zhao J. Intelligent sensing sensory quality of Chinese rice wine using near infrared spectroscopy and nonlinear tools. *Spectrochim Acta - Part A Mol Biomol Spectrosc* 2016;154:42–6.

Ouyang Q, Zhao J, Chen Q. Instrumental intelligent test of food sensory quality as mimic of human panel test combining multiple cross-perception sensors and data fusion. *Anal Chim Acta* 2014;841:68–76.

Ozer N, Engel BA, Simon JE. Fusion classification techniques for fruit quality. *Trans ASAE* 1995;38:1927–34.

Pan H, Okello N, Mcmichael D et al. *Fuzzy Causal Probabilistic Networks and Multisensor Data Fusion.* 1998;3543, DOI: 10.1117/12.323596.

Pasias IN, Kiriakou IK, Proestos C. HMF and diastase activity in honeys: A fully validated approach and a chemometric analysis for identification of honey freshness and adulteration. *Food Chem* 2017;229:425–31.

Peng B, Ge N, Cui L et al. Monitoring of alcohol strength and titratable acidity of apple wine during fermentation using near-infrared spectroscopy. *LWT - Food Sci Technol* 2016;66:86–92.

Pizarro C, Rodríguez-Tecedor S, Pérez-del-Notario N et al. Classification of Spanish extra virgin olive oils by data fusion of visible spectroscopic fingerprints and chemical descriptors. *Food Chem* 2013;138:915–22.

Pourkhak B, Mireei SA, Sadeghi M et al. Multi-sensor data fusion in the nondestructive measurement of kiwifruit texture. *Measurement* 2017;101:157–65.

Qiu S, Wang J. The prediction of food additives in the fruit juice based on electronic nose with chemometrics. *Food Chem* 2017;230:208–14.

Quinn L, Yaxley S, Knight JAG. Intelligent Monitoring for Quality of Fresh Citrus Fruit from Packing House to Supermarket. *Control Applications in Post-Harvest and Processing Technology.* 1995, 321.

Rajamäki T, Alakomi H-L, Ritvanen T et al. Application of an electronic nose for quality assessment of modified atmosphere packaged poultry meat. *Food Control* 2006;17:5–13.

Reis N, Botelho BG, Franca AS et al. Simultaneous Detection of Multiple Adulterants in Ground Roasted Coffee by ATR-FTIR Spectroscopy and Data Fusion. *Food Anal Methods* 2017:1–10.

Reis N, Franca AS, Oliveira LS. Performance of diffuse reflectance infrared Fourier transform spectroscopy and chemometrics for detection of multiple adulterants in roasted and ground coffee. *LWT - Food Sci Technol* 2013a;53:395–401.

Reis N, Franca AS, Oliveira LS. Discrimination between roasted coffee, roasted corn and coffee husks by Diffuse Reflectance Infrared Fourier Transform Spectroscopy. *LWT - Food Sci Technol* 2013b;50:715–22.

Rodriguez-Otero JL, Hermida M, Cepeda A. Determination of fat, protein, and total solids in cheese by near-infrared reflectance spectroscopy. *J AOAC Int* 1995;78:802–6.

Ros F, Guillaume S, Bellon-Maurel V. Classification of a Granular Product using High-Level Fusion of Vision Features. *J Agric Eng Res* 1997;68:115–24.

Roussel S, Bellon-Maurel V, Roger JM et al. Fusion of aroma, FT-IR and UV sensor data based on the Bayesian inference. Application to the discrimination of white grape varieties. *Chemom Intell Lab Syst* 2003;65:209–19.

Schlesier K, Fauhl-Hassek C, Forina M et al. Characterisation and determination of the geographical origin of wines. part i: Overview. *Eur Food Res Technol* 2009;230:1–13.

Schweizer-Berberich PM, Vaihinger S, Göpel W. Characterisation of food freshness with sensor arrays. *Sensors Actuators B Chem* 1994;18:282–90.

Sen I, Ozturk B, Tokatli F et al. Combination of visible and mid-infrared spectra for the prediction of chemical parameters of wines. *Talanta* 2016;161:130–7.

Silvestri M, Elia a., Bertelli D et al. A mid level data fusion strategy for the Varietal Classification of Lambrusco PDO wines. *Chemom Intell Lab Syst* 2014;137:181–9.

Sørensen KM, Khakimov B, Engelsen SB. The use of rapid spectroscopic screening methods to detect adulteration of food raw materials and ingredients. *Curr Opin Food Sci* 2016;10:45–51.

Spiteri M, Dubin E, Cotton J et al. Data fusion between high resolution 1H-NMR and mass spectrometry: a synergetic approach to honey botanical origin characterization. *Anal Bioanal Chem* 2016;408:4389–401.

Steinmetz V, Biavati E, Molto E et al. Predicting the maturity of oranges with non destructive sensors. *Actae Hortic* 1997;421:271–8.

Steinmetz V, Crochon M, Bellon Maurel V et al. Sensors for Fruit Firmness Assessment: Comparison and Fusion. *J Agric Eng Res* 1996;64:15–27.

Steinmetz V, Rabatel G, Crochon M et al. Sensor fusion for quality grading of melons. *Control Applications in Post-Harvest and Processing Technology*. 1995, 321.

Steinmetz V, Roger JM, Moltó E et al. On-line Fusion of Colour Camera and Spectrophotometer for Sugar Content Prediction of Apples. *J Agric Eng Res* 1999;73:207–16.

Steinmetz V, Sevila F, Bellon-Maurel V. A Methodology for sensor fusion design: Application to fruit quality assessment. *J Agric Eng Res* 1999;74:21–31.

Subari N, Saleh JM, Shakaff AYM et al. A hybrid sensing approach for pure and adulterated honey classification. *Sensors (Switzerland)* 2012;12:14022–40.

Throop JA, Rehkugler GE, Upchurch BL. *Application of Computer Vision for Detecting Watercore in Apples*. 1989;32, DOI: 10.13031/2013.31267.

Upchurch BL, Miles GE, Stroshine RL et al. *Ultrasonic Measurement for Detecting Apple Bruises*. 1987;30, DOI: 10.13031/2013.30478.

Wang W, Li C. A multimodal machine vision system for quality inspection of onions. *J Food Eng* 2015;166:291–301.

Wide P, Winquist F, Bergsten P et al. The human-based multisensor fusion method for artificial nose and tongue sensor data. *IEEE Trans Instrum Meas* 1998;47:1072–7.

Winquist F, Wide P, Eklov T et al. Crispbread Quality Evaluation Based on Fusion the Human Olfactory, Auditory and Tactile Senses. *J Food Process Eng* 1999;22:337–58.

Wu Z, Xu E, Long J et al. Comparison between ATR-IR, Raman, concatenated ATR-IR and Raman spectroscopy for the determination of total antioxidant capacity and total phenolic content of Chinese rice wine. *Food Chem* 2015;194:671–9.

Yamamoto H, Iwamoto M, Haginuma S. Acoustic impulse response method for measuring nautral frequency of intact fruits and preliminary applications to internal quality evaluation of apples and watermelons. *J Texture Stud* 1980;11:117–36.

Yamamoto H, Iwamoto M, Haginuma S. Nondestructive acoustic impulse response method for measuring internal quality of apples and watermelons. *J Japanese Soc Hortic Sci* 1981;50:247–61.

Yang R, Dong G, Sun X et al. Synchronous–asynchronous two-dimensional correlation spectroscopy for the discrimination of adulterated milk. *Anal Methods* 2015;7:4302–7.

Yongwei W, Wang J, Zhou B et al. Monitoring storage time and quality attribute of egg based on electronic nose. *Anal Chim Acta* 2009;650:183–8.

Zhang S, Xie C, Bai Z et al. Spoiling and formaldehyde-containing detections in octopus with an E-nose. *Food Chem* 2009;113:1346–50.

Zheng C, Sun D-W, Zheng L. Recent applications of image texture for evaluation of food qualities—a review. *Trends Food Sci Technol* 2006;17:113–28.

Zhong YS, Ni YN, Kokot S. Application of differential pulse stripping voltammetry and chemometrics for the determination of three antibiotic drugs in food samples. *Chinese Chem Lett* 2012;23:339–42.

Zhu W, Wang X, Chen L. Rapid detection of peanut oil adulteration using low-field nuclear magnetic resonance and chemometrics. *Food Chem* 2017;216:268–74.

In: Data Fusion
Editors: V. Albert and E. Aba

ISBN: 978-1-53612-720-1
© 2017 Nova Science Publishers, Inc.

Chapter 3

MATHEMATICAL ASPECTS OF DATA FUSION IN MULTIPLE SEARCH AND TRACKING SYSTEMS

Carlo Quaranta and *Giorgio Balzarotti*

Leonardo S.p.a, Radar and Advanced Targeting LoB,
IRST BA, Nerviano (MI), Italy

ABSTRACT

The problem for a data fusion system of a non-exhaustive number of common measurements from sensors of different types is faced here. In the presence of a suite of heterogeneous sensors, the data fusion process has to deal with the management of different information that is generally not directly comparable. Hence, the process of association and fusion between the data of tracks from different sensors is complicated by the fact of having a limited number of comparable measurements: also, objects located at a great distance from each other can give rise to wrong associations between them. The analysis is carried out considering the

---

[*] Corresponding Author Email: carlo.quaranta@leonardocompany.com.

fusion of data between radar and Infrared Search and Track (IRST) where the measurement of the range is achieved by radar only and demonstrates the need for a tracking process of the fused tracks that allows the effective use of algorithms such as, for example, the Joint Probabilistic Data Association (JPDA) in order to reduce the probability of bad associations between tracks from different sensors. Moreover, because of the tracking process of the fused tracks, it is suggested to use a new fusion equation that exploits the characteristics of the sensors in use that performs better in the presence of fast variation of the state of the tracks from the different sensors. Simulation results demonstrate the effectiveness of the algorithms, specifically the fusion process, tracking and correctness of association among tracks from different sensors. A comparison between the new fusion equation and a known approach from the literature is also performed.

Keywords: data fusion, radar, IRST, JPDA

1. INTRODUCTION

Sensors with different behaviors and technologies collect multiple diverse aspects of reality. Working together, they can provide a deep analysis of the operational scenario and increase situational awareness.

But diversity also means different outputs in terms of quantities, resolution, reliability, consistency, extension and range. The information collected by the different sensors could be fully redundant or, simply and more commonly, qualitatively redundant, it can include measurements of the same quantities, but with different accuracy and band or different measurements altogether. This diversity can sometimes make it difficult, or simply not cost effective, to obtain a beneficial fusion of data.

This chapter will attempt to analyze these kinds of problems and provides methods to cope with them. The detailed analysis is limited to the fusion of data from *Search and Track Systems,* the most common of which are the *RADAR* and the *IRST*, but the proposed mathematics can also be extended to many other more general and broader situations.

In fusion of *Search and Track Systems*, one of the key aspects is the association of detections or tracks to the same physical object. Especially in an operational scenario, the targets could be close to one another, or distributed in such a way to obscure their threat level. A precise association of the detections or tracks from different sensors is, in this case, of paramount importance for the success of the fusion process and of the mission.

After a description in general terms and an explanation of the mathematical approach, an analysis is carried out considering the fusion of data between RADAR and IRST. The method of data fusion is clearly shown for these sensors that provide heterogeneous measurements, since the RADAR provides an accurate range but a limited accuracy in angles, while the IRST performs an approximate evaluation of the range or, as often it happens, it does not provide any range information at all, but keeps a precise angular position of tracks.

For reducing the probability of bad associations between close tracks, the *Joint Probabilistic Data Association (JPDA)* is tailored specifically for data fusion. To improve the tracking process of the fused tracks in the presence of fast variation, specific fusion equation s are suggested and described.

2. BASIC PRINCIPLES

Let us assume we have M sensors. S*ensors,* for our purpose, are physical apparatus, i.e., electronic equipment able to perform some specific *measurements and estimations* of *reality*. Reality is the *environment* where the sensors are located.

The *measurements* are performed by collecting electromagnetic radiations, acoustic waves, temperatures, acceleration... in a fully passive way or after an active and controlled emission, for example, of incoherent electromagnetic pulses or laser pulses.

The M sensors are not necessarily all different. They could be all of the same kind and nature or partially equivalent. In principle they could be located in the same environment or far from each other i.e., they can observe the same *scene* or different scenes. The *points of observation* of the scene can be physically different.

Within the wide set of measurements the sensor can acquire about the scene, we assume that some of those are related to a *class of objects of interest.* We refer to these objects as *targets.*

Objects that are not targets fall under the category of background, noise, clutter or foreground... *Background, noise, clutter, foreground* help in some cases in finding targets, but they are not *objects of interest.*

The *M* sensors and the associate electronics and processors to perform measurements constitute the *systems.* The *status* or *state* of the system is a collection of variables able to describe the behavior of the system over time.

The *class of objects of interest* is defined and described by means of precise *statements.* The fusion algorithms must be tailored following those *statements.*

The *system,* for our purpose, has the task to extract as much as possible precise and reliable information about *targets.*

We will focus, in our work, on the determination of a *track*, a series of kinematic data related to the motion of the target of interest (status). The collection of a sequence of track data over time constitutes the trajectory of the target.

The trajectory is assumed to be requested in *real time* by the systems. *Real time,* for our purpose, means that the delay of the *system* in providing a trajectory is *small* with respect to the *dynamics* of *all objects of interest.*

It is also important to note that each sensor can have its own time and measurement update rate which is normally different to the others.

Even if the following description can be applied in general, we will restrict the analysis by assuming that each sensor, and the relevant processor, performs search, detection and tracking of targets and autonomously provides, or simply it tries to provide, the *target tracks.*

The task of sensor and data fusion is to manage the outputs of the *M* processors to give, for all targets in the scene, integrated, reliable, precise and exhaustive estimations of the targets trajectories.

Figure 1 represents the system composed of M sensors, M sensors processors and the *data fusion system* [2].

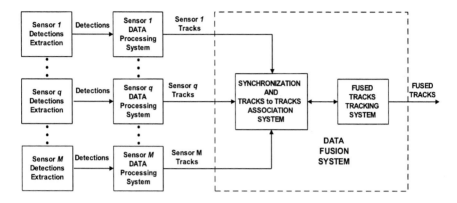

Figure 1. General block diagram of a Data Fusion System.

3. GENERAL DEFINITION OF THE CONTEXT FOR SENSORS DATA FUSION

Any measurement is affected by noise and errors. We will assume that measurements and estimations have zero mean value Gaussian probability density function (*pdf*). In some cases we will remove those limitations.

Measurements are generally sampled in time and are managed with discrete time processors. In general, the scene is, as well, space and/or time sampled by subsequent *swaths or frames*.

Let us designate with T_s the scanning period, the swath or frame period or, generically, the *scenario revisit time* of one sensor belonging to the set of sensors. So, the time is no longer continuous and we may write $t = k \cdot T_s$, where the integer k is the counter.

If we decide to identify the *tracks* with the *status* of the system, we can write the status simply by

$$x(k) = x(k \cdot T_s) = x(t)\big|_{t = k \cdot T_s}$$

thus removing, with the notation on the left, time from the equations.

We have a *status* at the output of each one of the *M sensors*, therefore *M tracks,* at most, for a single target.

In general we have $N \leq M$ *tracks*. The reason of inequality symbol derives from many factors, mainly:

- the performances or, more simply, the characteristics of some sensors are not adequate for detecting the target
- some sensors are observing different scenes
- revisit times of some sensors are not consistent with target dynamics (i.e., the sampling time is too low)

On the contrary the equal condition does not necessary mean that all sensors are tracking the same target because

- not all the trajectories reconstructed by the *M* sensors are properly associated to the same target

Also, we have to note that we could have a specific *scenario revisit time* for each sensor and T_s could be selected, for example, to approximate the less common divisor of all revisits time. This approach does not anyway guarantee the phasing of the measurements collected by the different sensors.

Let us assume, in what follows, that samplings are synchronized through any technique [1].

The aim is now to use the *N* estimates from the *M* sensors for the best reconstruction of the target trajectory in the scene fully or partially covered by the *M* sensors.

3.1. Track to Track Association Process

Let x_q and x_r be the states of two tracks from sensors q and r, we can say without doubts that they are linked to the same object if and only if it results, in the absence of offsets:

$$x_r(t) = x_q(t) \quad \forall t \tag{1}$$

It is obviously clear that, due to the measurement and process noises, the above relationship is never verified and a more realistic case is:

$$x_r(t) \approx x_q(t) \quad \forall t$$

The relationship is only apparently trivial because it is the source of the main issues in the field of sensor fusion:

- if the relationship stands in all conditions, it means one of the two sensors is fully redundant. Does the redundant one increase only the cost and the complexity of the system?
- the symbol $\approx$ indicates that one or the other status, or more probably both, do not perfectly track the trajectory of the target. Whatever the accuracy of an estimate with respect to the real target trajectory, why not use both estimates to achieve a better fit of the real target trajectory and thus approach the theoretic perfect tracking?

In this chapter we do not deal with problems related to the cost, but we focus on gaining the maximum benefit from the information coming from the N states in spite of the cost. Thus we will try to give a positive follow up to the second question by using all sensors available to the system.

When introducing that topic, we considered sensors using very different technology such as electromagnetic or acoustic. It is quite natural to assume that the states relevant to the target trajectories, generated by different sensors, have different accuracy or content. We can also assume that the target motion cannot be fully determined by some sensors of the set. A typical example is the lack of range measurement in the status of a passive electro-optical system.

For the moment, let us consider that the measurements made by all sensors are *commensurable*, i.e., that all sensors could provide the measurements of the same quantities (i.e., distances of the targets, angles with respect the point of view), and let denote with $x_1, x_2, \cdots, x_M$ the states related to the M tracks from the M sensors (one track for each sensor). Let us designate by

$$\Delta x_{qr}(k) = x_q(k) - x_r(k) \tag{2}$$

the vector *distance* between the states of two tracks from the sensors q and r at the time $k \cdot T_s$.

We indicate with $P_{qr} = E\{\Delta x_{qr} \cdot \Delta x_{qr}^T\}$ the cross covariance matrix of the distance Δx_{qr}, where $E\{\ \}$, as usual, is the expected value of the quantity in brackets and the symbol ^{T} indicates the vector/matrix transpose operation.

The vector of all the distances, combining each of the M states with all the others M-1 states, is:

$$\Delta x^T(k) = \left[\underbrace{\Delta x_{12}(k) \cdots \ \Delta x_{1M}(k)}_{M-1} \underbrace{\Delta x_{23}(k) \cdots \ \Delta x_{2M}(k)}_{M-2} \cdots \underbrace{\Delta x_{qq+1}(k) \cdots \ \Delta x_{qM}(k)}_{M-q} \cdots \Delta x_{M-1M}(k) \right] \tag{3}$$

The *cross covariance matrix* relative to the entire cross distances is:

$$P = E\{\Delta x \cdot \Delta x^T\} \tag{4}$$

where the expected value is computed over each element of the matrix and along the history of the process.

If the state of each track is defined by d dimensions, the size of the vector Δx will be $D = d \cdot M \cdot \dfrac{M-1}{2}$ and D^2 the size of the cross covariance matrix P.

It is well known that the *matrix P* of the *cross covariance* is *non negative definite*, and that the determinant of P is null only if two or more sets of measurements are not linearly independent. In all the other cases we can compute the scalar:

$$\Delta x^T(k) \cdot P^{-1} \cdot \Delta x(k)$$

Some consideration about the achieved figure:

- It assumes zero value if and only if $\Delta x(k) \equiv 0$
- A zero value means that the M sensors are perfectly sampling, at instant k, the same trajectory
- A zero value does not mean the tracked trajectory is exactly the target trajectory, because there is no real target trajectory as reference in the formula.
- A constant offset over all measurements does not provide any effect on the achieved value, but will produce bias in the estimation error that could lead to the loss of the fused tracks. Offsets are to be managed separately. We have assumed at the beginning of the description, that measurements and estimations have zero mean value Gaussian *pdf.*
- A zero value is surely unrealistic in practice, however, a "small" value for *total distances covariance* shows that the M sensors are providing a good fit of the target motion at k.

From the above considerations, we can accept the hypothesis that the M tracks from the M sensors concern the same object if:

$$\Delta x^T(k) \cdot P^{-1} \cdot \Delta x(k) < \gamma \qquad \forall k \qquad (5)$$

γ being a suitable scalar value.

In this case, γ plays the role of *threshold* in discriminating the consistency of the tracks from the M sensors.

It is important to note now that the left hand side of (5) is equivalent to the sum of squares of D independent zero mean-unity-variance Gaussian random variables (the variables $\Delta x(k)$ are not).

It is well know that the sum of squares of D independent normal random variable has a chi-square distribution (χ^2 pdf) with D degrees of freedom. That is an important result because it enables us to select γ by using the χ^2 tables, one of the main tools in the area of statistical interference and hypothesis testing. We will return later on the definition of γ.

The calculation of the matrix P is generally quite complex and expensive compared to the other computation we have to cope with, therefore it is useful to look for some simplifications.

The *distances of states* of different couples of sensors could be assumed having zero correlation [9] or, which is equivalent, be independent.

Therefore for some of the M states we can assume:

$$P_{qrmn} = E\left\{\Delta x_{qr} \cdot \Delta x_{mn}^{T}\right\} \equiv 0 \tag{6}$$

In this case, the correlation matrix P becomes a block diagonal matrix.

For that, and especially in the general case of sensors with a non-exhaustive set of commensurable measurements/estimates, it is reasonable to separately analyze couples of sensors.

To simplify the description, let us consider two sensors only, 1 and 2, and N commensurable measurements/estimates.

Let N_s be the number of quantities we need to represent the target's motion (N_s could be simply 3 for a 3D tracking) and let N be the commensurable measurements (measurements of same kinds) from sensors 1 and 2 (two angles for example). Note that it is good practice to use all information available and that N_s is equal or greater than the order of the set achieved by the union of the sets of all direct measurements.

Now we have to introduce an important issue: to apply the equation (5) we need, in some way, to *build* the N_s - N missing measurements /estimates. One of the methods is to keep the missing ones from the sensor 2, for instance, from the status of the sensor 1, and vice versa for the missing ones from sensor 1. In this way we can build a new status of the track represented by the same order N_s of state variables.

Now, because it is expected to have more than one track from both sensors and, clearly, the true association is unknown, the process of *sharing* measurements/estimates in the states of the tracks of the two sensors must be performed for all the possible tracks. The process will be clearer in the next step.

With the above method we will have:

- the use of all information given by the different sensors (no direct measurement is missing)
- a space of trajectories, created by sharing and blending measurements, which includes, in theory, all the true target trajectories.
- a criteria to discriminate the true target trajectories among the space of the possible trajectories, thanks to the applicability of the formula (5).

Returning to the simplest cases of two sensors, said x_1 and x_2 the states of two tracks and N_s their new dimensions; we rewrite equation (5) as:

$$\Delta x_{12}^T(k) \cdot P_{12}^{-1} \cdot \Delta x_{12}(k) < \gamma \qquad \forall k \text{ in a proper interval} \qquad (7)$$

Now we need to investigate how to use the above results.

First of all, we introduce, as usual in all practical cases, the symbols of estimations of the status of a track $\hat{x}(k|k)$ as the estimate for the current time and $\hat{x}(k+1|k)$ as the prediction for the next frame, given the history up to the current frame. The condition "$\forall k$ in a proper interval" has to be read that (7) have to be repeated over k frames.

Equation (7) is necessary in theory, however, because an initial screening can be derived by considering that two tracks are potentially related to the same object if, for all N commensurable measurements/estimates of the status, the following condition will stand:

$$\mu_q = \left| \hat{x}_{1q}(k|k) - \hat{x}_{2q}(k|k) \right| < \lambda_q \qquad q = 1,2,...,N \tag{8}$$

where $\hat{x}_{sq}(k|k)$ is the q-th component of the state estimation from the sensor s.

λ_q can be defined by considering that the absolute value of the difference of two uncorrelated random variable with zero mean value and Gaussian distribution will have a non-Gaussian distribution with expected value and variance given by

$$\begin{cases} m = E\{\mu_q\} = \sqrt{\dfrac{2}{\pi}} \cdot (\sigma_{1q} + \sigma_{2q}) \\[2mm] \sigma^2 = E\{(\mu_q - m)^2\} = \dfrac{\pi - 2}{\pi} \cdot (\sigma_{1b}^2 + \sigma_{2b}^2) \le \dfrac{\pi - 2}{2} \cdot m^2 \end{cases} \tag{9}$$

where σ_{1q}^2 and σ_{2q}^2 are the variances of the q-th component of the two state variable. With the above values we can evaluate the *risk* that the two states are related to the same object when they are not, as well as to consider them associated to different objects when they are related to the same.

In practical cases the status is not directly the output of the sensors, but it passes through a linear or non-linear transformation. Let us indicate with $f_q[\hat{x}_1(k|k), \hat{x}_2(k|k)]$ and $g_q[\hat{x}_1(k|k), \hat{x}_2(k|k)]$ the transformation of the q-th element of the status, respectively for the first and second sensors.

We can construct the matrix:

$$\Omega(k) = \begin{bmatrix} \hat{\xi}_1(k|k) & \hat{\xi}_2(k|k) \end{bmatrix} = \begin{bmatrix} f_1[\hat{x}_1(k|k), \hat{x}_2(k|k)] & g_1[\hat{x}_1(k|k), \hat{x}_2(k|k)] \\ f_2[\hat{x}_1(k|k), \hat{x}_2(k|k)] & g_2[\hat{x}_1(k|k), \hat{x}_2(k|k)] \\ f_3[\hat{x}_1(k|k), \hat{x}_2(k|k)] & g_3[\hat{x}_1(k|k), \hat{x}_2(k|k)] \\ \vdots & \vdots \\ f_{N_s}[\hat{x}_1(k|k), \hat{x}_2(k|k)] & g_{N_s}[\hat{x}_1(k|k), \hat{x}_2(k|k)] \end{bmatrix} \tag{10}$$

$\Omega(k)$ becomes, in general case, the input for the test (7) (a particular condition is when the two transformations are identical or unitary).

Let us now designate $P_1 = E\{\Delta\xi_1(k)\cdot\Delta\xi_1^T(k)\}$ and $P_2 = E\{\Delta\xi_2(k)\cdot\Delta\xi_2^T(k)\}$ as the matrices of covariance of the estimation error on $\hat{\xi}_1$ and $\hat{\xi}_2$, respectively, the cross covariance matrix of the difference $\hat{\xi}_1(k|k) - \hat{\xi}_2(k|k)$ will be given by:

$$P = E\left\{\left[\hat{\xi}_1(k|k) - \hat{\xi}_2(k|k)\right]\cdot\left[\hat{\xi}_1(k|k) - \hat{\xi}_2(k|k)\right]^T\right\} = P_1 + P_2 - C_{12} - C_{12}^T \qquad (11)$$

where $C_{12} = E\{\Delta\xi_1(k)\cdot\Delta\xi_2^T(k)\} = C_{21}^T$.

We obtain:

$$\left[\hat{\xi}_1(k|k) - \hat{\xi}_2(k|k)\right]^T \cdot P^{-1} \cdot \left[\hat{\xi}_1(k|k) - \hat{\xi}_2(k|k)\right] < \gamma_0 \qquad (12)$$

(which is the (7)) where γ_0 can be appropriately chosen by using the tables of χ^2.

We define *mixed detections* as the matrix $\Omega(k)$. The name detection derives from similarity with tracking systems where the detection are the inputs of the process while *mixed* clearly derives from the fact that detection is obtained by mixing the data from two different sensors.

3.2. The Fusion equation

The mixed detection $\Omega(k)$ provides two different estimations of the state of the target of interest meaning that one of them could be redundant. So the questions are:

1. How convenient is it to fuse the data from the sensors?

Indeed there is no definitive answer to this question, but it is all left to the common sense of the designer who will decide on a case by case basis. However, when the differences of the estimation errors are much greater than one order of growth, the contribution of the less accurate sensor to the estimations becomes superfluous.

2. How can we use both the estimates to get a better fit of the real target motion?

As a matter of fact the columns of the mixed detection $\Omega(k)$ provides $\hat{\xi}_1(k|k)$ and $\hat{\xi}_2(k|k)$ that are the estimations of the same quantity, probably with different estimation errors, as seen by the two sensors by the use of mixed data as described above for the missing measurements. Dropping the time argument for simplicity, a usual way to get the data fusion $\hat{x}(\Omega)$ of $\hat{\xi}_1$ and $\hat{\xi}_2$ is through the following fusion equation (see Chapter   9   of [5, 8]):

$$\hat{x}(\Omega) = \hat{\xi}_2 + A \cdot \left(\hat{\xi}_1 - \hat{\xi}_2 \right) = A \cdot \hat{\xi}_1 + (I - A) \cdot \hat{\xi}_2 \tag{13}$$

with I identity matrix and A to be properly found. Since we want to have the best possible estimate of $\hat{x}(\Omega)$, we select A in such a way to minimize the mean square error $\Delta x(\Omega)$ along all the components of $\hat{x}(\Omega)$. To do that, A is chosen to minimize the trace of the covariance matrix $P_\Omega = E\left\{ \Delta x(\Omega) \cdot \Delta x^T(\Omega) \right\}$ of the error on $\hat{x}(\Omega)$. As a matter of fact, since the trace of P_Ω is the sum of the mean square error in the estimates of the elements of $\hat{x}(\Omega)$ we can argue that the individual mean square errors are also minimized, minimizing the latter sum. Now with $\Delta\xi_1$, $\Delta\xi_2$, P, P_1, P_2 and C_{12} as previously defined, Equation (13) can now be rewritten in form of the aforementioned errors as:

$$\Delta x(\Omega) = \Delta \xi_2 + A \cdot (\Delta \xi_1 - \Delta \xi_2)$$

with covariance matrix:

$$P_\Omega = P_2 + A \cdot (C_{12} - P_2) + [A \cdot (C_{12} - P_2)]^T + A \cdot P \cdot A^T \tag{14}$$

To minimize the trace of P_Ω now we have to take the derivative of the trace of (14) with respect to the matrix A and then force it to zero. Before proceeding further, we recall some matrix differentiation rules. Let us designate three square matrices, X, Y and Z, where Z is symmetric.
It is:

$$\frac{d[trace(X \cdot Y)]}{dX} = Y^T,$$

$$\frac{d[trace(X \cdot Z \cdot X^T)]}{dX} = 2 \cdot X \cdot Z$$

and the derivative of a scalar a with respect to a matrix $X = [x_{qr}]$, with $q = 1,2,\cdots,N$ $r = 1,2,\cdots,N$, is defined as:

$$\frac{d[a]}{dX} = \begin{bmatrix} \dfrac{da}{dx_{11}} & \dfrac{da}{dx_{12}} & \cdots \\ \dfrac{da}{dx_{21}} & \dfrac{da}{dx_{22}} & \cdots \\ \vdots & \vdots & \vdots \end{bmatrix}$$

Since P is a symmetrical matrix, applying the previous differentiation rules to (14) it is:

$$\frac{d[trace(P_\Omega)]}{dA} = 2 \cdot (C_{12} - P_2)^T + 2 \cdot A \cdot P$$

and equating it to zero we finally get:

$$A = (P_2 - C_{12})^T \cdot P^{-1} \qquad (15)$$

The matrix A, being a "ratio" between the variance of one sensor with respect to the total one, performs a weighting operation on the data provided by all sensors. The result is that the output of the fusion is driven by the data which has least estimation error. Nevertheless, A is obtained through the use of the covariance matrices P, P_2 and C_{12} whose elements are the output of a low pass filtering process, since they were obtained through a mean in the time ($P_\Omega = E\{ \}$). This implies that matrix A has low dynamics and it is not suitable to represent changes in the motion of targets or changes sometimes simply due to noise. On the contrary we expect that the fusion system should be able to react quickly to any, even small, changes in the motion of the target so maintaining the proper track-to-track associations and hence the stability of the fused tracks. In specific conditions, one sensor could better perform against changes than the others and such behavior shall be exploited by the data fusion process.

A relatively different approach [1, 3], which does not exhibit the same drawback, is to reformulate the matrix A. We can write

$$\hat{x}(\Omega) = \alpha \cdot \hat{\xi}_1 + (1-\alpha) \cdot \hat{\xi}_2 \qquad (16)$$

where α is as scalar given by

$$\alpha = \frac{G_1}{G_1 + G_2} \qquad (17)$$

and

$$
\begin{cases}
G_1 = \dfrac{e^{-\frac{1}{2}\left(\hat{\xi}_1 - \hat{z}\right)^T \cdot S^{-1} \cdot \left(\hat{\xi}_1 - \hat{z}\right)}}{\sqrt{(2\pi)^n \cdot |S|}} \\[3ex]
G_2 = \dfrac{e^{-\frac{1}{2}\left(\hat{\xi}_2 - \hat{z}\right)^T \cdot S^{-1} \cdot \left(\hat{\xi}_2 - \hat{z}\right)}}{\sqrt{(2\pi)^n \cdot |S|}}
\end{cases}
\tag{18}
$$

where $\hat{z} = \hat{z}(k|k-1)$ is the *predicted measure* for the current frame k, evaluated at the previous one by the fused tracks tracking system (see Figure 1). $S = E\{v(k) \cdot v^T(k)\}$ is the covariance matrix of the residue $v(k) = \xi - \hat{z}(k|k-1)$ of the *measure* ξ received by the fusion system with respect to $\hat{z}$ (the predicted one).

Equation (16), in contrary to (13), uses the instantaneous errors $\hat{\xi}_1 - \hat{z}$ and $\hat{\xi}_2 - \hat{z}$ instead of average values for the estimation of $\hat{x}(\Omega)$ and therefore performs better behaviors to quick variations. The covariance matrix R of $\hat{x}(\Omega)$ is now:

$$
R = \alpha^2 \cdot P_1 + (1-\alpha)^2 \cdot P_2 + \alpha \cdot (1-\alpha) \cdot \left(C_{12} + C_{12}^T\right).
$$

To prove what is stated above, let us analyze the following example. Two sensors, a RADAR and an IRST, are used to observe a target that linearly moves starting from a distance of about 70 Km which approaches the observer at a constant altitude and with a constant speed of *250 km/h*. The noise is determined solely by the error of measurements as the target trajectory is linear. The root mean square (rms) measurement error of the RADAR's range is *75 m*. For the angular errors, we consider three different cases 0.5 degrees, 0.75 degrees and 1 degree rms. The measurement noise of IRST is assumed to be 0.035 degrees for azimuth and elevation, no range measurement available. For each case, we have performed 5 runs. During each simulation, we measured the probability of the gate of the fused track and the number of times the track was lost and reacquired. In Table 3.1, the validation probability is estimated as the ratio $p = \dfrac{N_a}{N_F}$, being N_a the number of times that the gate validates a mixed detection, N_F the number of frames in the lifetime of the fused track.

Figure 2 (a) shows, as a function of time, the total error during a run (no track loss happened in the run) performed with the fusion equation (13), while Figure 2 (b) shows the total estimation error resulted from the use of equation (16). The peaks of errors in Figure 2 (a) derive from the inability of equation (16) to properly react to the measurement noise. Comparing Figures 2 (a) and 2 (b) in the region where there is not this instability, we observe that, even if the new fusion equation does not derive from optimization criteria, the errors are comparable.

The error is computed by $\varepsilon(k) = \sqrt{\varepsilon_x^2(k) + \varepsilon_y^2(k) + \varepsilon_z^2(k)}$, with ε_x, ε_y and ε_z errors along the coordinates axes.

Table 3.1 summarizes the results of all runs with the two different fusion equation s [2].

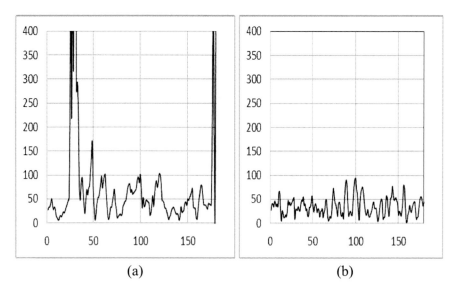

(a)　　　　　　　　　　　　　　　(b)

Figure 2. Total estimation error (m): (a) Fusion equation (13); (b) Fusion equation (16).

Table 3.1. Summary of the results of all runs

Angular measurement rms error (degrees)	RUNs	Fusion equation (13)		Proposed Fusion equation (16)	
		Validation Probability	Number of Lost Tracks	Validation Probability	Number of Lost Tracks
Azimuth error = 0.5	1	0.73	1	1	0
Elevation error = 0.5	2	0.72	0	0.9868	0
	3	0.74	0	0.9954	0
	4	0.72	2	0.9955	0
	5	0.73	5	1	0
Azimuth error = 0.75	6	0.65	9	1	0
Elevation error = 0.75	7	0.67	8	0.9958	0
	8	0.91	0	1	0
	9	0.70	5	1	0
	10	0.72	2	1	0
Azimuth error = 1.0	11	0.64	8	1	0
Elevation error = 1.0	12	0.65	5	1	0
	13	0.70	7	1	0
	14	0.64	7	1	0
	15	0.65	5	1	0

3.3. Mixed detections to Fused Tracks Association and Tracking

Whichever fusion equation is used, a mixed detection is associated to the gate of a given fused track if the following χ^2 test is verified:

$$\left[\hat{x}(\Omega) - \hat{z}(k|k-1)\right]^T \cdot S^{-1} \cdot \left[\hat{x}(\Omega) - \hat{z}(k|k-1)\right] < \gamma \qquad (19)$$

where $\hat{z} = \hat{z}(k|k-1)$ is *predicted measure* and $S = E\{v(k) \cdot v^T(k)\}$ is the covariance matrix of the residue.

In the case where (19) is not verified, $\hat{x}(\Omega)$ does not belong to the relevant fused track and it could be used to initiate a new fused track. On the contrary, $\hat{x}(\Omega)$ *could belong* to the relevant fused track. Correct association is not guaranteed because the incompleteness of the data available from the different sensors could lead the association of a track of one sensor to more than one track of the other. That is an *undesired track-to-track association*. We will investigate the issue, after the next case study.

4. A CASE STUDY: RADAR-IRST DATA FUSION

Let us come back to the case of RADAR and IRST detection and tracking fusion.

The RADAR carries out measurements of range, azimuth and elevation, while the IRST azimuth and elevation and we assume all measurements are independent. With the method described, azimuth and elevation are what we call *common measurements*.

For simplifying the description, we assume the data from the sensors are synchronized. T_s is the scan period and the inputs of the IRST (i.e., the "measurements" made by the sensor) are:

- azimuth $\varphi(k)$
- elevation $\vartheta(k)$

as well as the inputs for RADAR are:

- range $r(k)$
- azimuth $\beta(k)$
- elevation $\eta(k)$

The top level block diagram of the system under analysis is shown in Figure 3.

The outputs of the IRST are:

- State estimation and prediction: $\left[\hat{\varphi}(k\,|\,k),\hat{\vartheta}(k\,|\,k)\right]$, $\left[\hat{\varphi}(k+1\,|\,k),\hat{\vartheta}(k+1\,|\,k)\right]$.

- State error estimation and prediction: $\sigma_{\varphi}^{2}(k\,|\,k)$, $\sigma_{\vartheta}^{2}(k\,|\,k)$ and $\sigma_{\varphi}^{2}(k+1\,|\,k)$, $\sigma_{\vartheta}^{2}(k+1\,|\,k)$.

With regard to the RADAR data processor, the direct use of spherical measurements will produce a nonlinear system of equations that requires the use of an Extended Kalman Filter (EKF). Here we assume RADAR processor operates in the Cartesian coordinates system. The conversion from spherical to Cartesian coordinates is reached by:

$$\begin{cases} x(k) = r(k) \cdot \cos[\beta(k)] \cdot \cos[\eta(k)] \\ y(k) = r(k) \cdot \sin[\beta(k)] \cdot \cos[\eta(k)] \\ z(k) = r(k) \cdot \sin[\eta(k)] \end{cases} \tag{20}$$

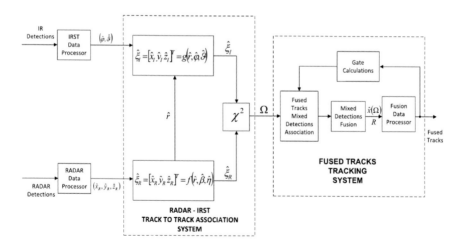

Figure 3. Block diagram of the RADAR-IRST Data Fusion System.

With this transformation the state equation will be linear and can therefore be handled by an ordinary Kalman filter. It is known (see Chapter 1 of [5]) that this conversion produces correlation among the converted data and bias on the error of the transformed measurements. These issues can be managed (see approaches in [1, 5]) resulting in the following outputs from the data processor of the RADAR:

- State estimate: $\left[\hat{x}_R(k\,|\,k), \hat{y}_R(k\,|\,k), \hat{z}_R(k\,|\,k)\right]$;

- State prediction: $\left[\hat{x}_R(k+1\,|\,k), \hat{y}_R(k+1\,|\,k), \hat{z}_R(k+1\,|\,k)\right]$;

- Estimate and prediction of the variances of the state error: $\sigma_x^2 = E\{\Delta x_R^2\}$, $\sigma_y^2 = E\{\Delta y_R^2\}$ and $\sigma_z^2 = E\{\Delta z_R^2\}$, being Δx_R, Δy_R e Δz_R the estimation errors along the coordinates axes.

- Estimate and prediction of the cross correlation among the state errors: $\rho_{xy} = E\{\Delta x_R \cdot \Delta y_R\}$, $\rho_{xz} = E\{\Delta x_R \cdot \Delta z_R\}$ and $\rho_{yz} = E\{\Delta y_R \cdot \Delta z_R\}$

In the fusion processor, to implement the association tests we have to perform the following transformation in order to make comparable the angular data of the two sensors:

$$\begin{cases} \hat{r} = \sqrt{\hat{x}_R^2 + \hat{y}_R^2 + \hat{z}_R^2} \\ \hat{r}_{xy} = \sqrt{\hat{x}_R^2 + \hat{y}_R^2} \\ \hat{\beta} = arctg\left(\dfrac{\hat{y}_R}{\hat{x}_R}\right) \\ \hat{\eta} = arctg\left(\dfrac{\hat{z}_R}{\hat{r}_{xy}}\right) \end{cases} \tag{21}$$

$\hat{r}_{xy}$ being the estimation of the projection onto the XY plane of the observer-target line. The statistics of data are derived in Appendix A.

4.1. Track-to-Track Association, Fusion and Tracking Process

The angles $\hat{\beta}, \hat{\eta}$ from the RADAR and $\hat{\varphi}$, $\hat{\vartheta}$ from the IRST, are the *common measurements*. Their distances vector has to pass the condition (7) for the track-to-track association process. So we proceed with the following *steps*:

For all the tracks from RADAR and IRST the following tests are performed:

$$
\begin{cases}
\left|\hat{\varphi}(k|k) - \hat{\beta}(k|k)\right| < K_A \cdot \varepsilon_A \\
\left|\hat{\vartheta}(k|k) - \hat{\eta}(k|k)\right| < K_E \cdot \varepsilon_E
\end{cases}
\tag{22}
$$

with $\varepsilon_A = \sigma_\varphi + \sigma_\beta$ and $\varepsilon_E = \sigma_\vartheta + \sigma_\eta$. The constants K_A and K_E are selected using (9).

For all the tracks that have passed test (22), we proceed to create the mixed detection Ω, with $\hat{r}$, the estimated track range from the RADAR:

$$
\Omega = \begin{bmatrix} \hat{\xi}_I & \hat{\xi}_R \end{bmatrix} = \begin{bmatrix} \hat{x}_I & \hat{x}_R \\ \hat{y}_I & \hat{y}_R \\ \hat{z}_I & \hat{z}_R \end{bmatrix} = \begin{bmatrix} \hat{r} \cdot \cos\hat{\varphi} \cdot \cos\hat{\vartheta} & \hat{r} \cdot \cos\hat{\beta} \cdot \cos\hat{\eta} \\ \hat{r} \cdot \sin\hat{\varphi} \cdot \cos\hat{\vartheta} & \hat{r} \cdot \sin\hat{\beta} \cdot \cos\hat{\eta} \\ \hat{r} \cdot \sin\hat{\vartheta} & \hat{r} \cdot \sin\hat{\eta} \end{bmatrix}
\tag{23}
$$

(For the statistical relations of the various terms of Ω see [1]. Appendix B provides the correlations between the errors $\Delta\xi_I$ and $\Delta\xi_R$).

We can now verify the condition (7):

$$
\left(\hat{\xi}_R - \hat{\xi}_I\right)^T \cdot P^{-1} \cdot \left(\hat{\xi}_R - \hat{\xi}_I\right) < \gamma
\tag{24}
$$

with γ chosen by using the ordinary tables of χ^2 and

$$
P = P_R + P_I - C_{RI} - C_{IR}
\tag{25}
$$

P_R is the covariance matrix of the estimation error provided by the RADAR Data Processor, and

$$P_I = \begin{bmatrix} \sigma^2_{x_I} & E\{\Delta x_I \cdot \Delta y_I\} & E\{\Delta x_I \cdot \Delta z_I\} \\ E\{\Delta x_I \cdot \Delta y_I\} & \sigma^2_{y_I} & E\{\Delta y_I \cdot \Delta z_I\} \\ E\{\Delta x_I \cdot \Delta z_I\} & E\{\Delta y_I \cdot \Delta z_I\} & \sigma^2_{z_I} \end{bmatrix} \tag{26}$$

and

$$C_{RI} = \begin{bmatrix} E\{\Delta x_R \cdot \Delta x_I\} & E\{\Delta x_R \cdot \Delta y_I\} & E\{\Delta x_R \cdot \Delta z_I\} \\ E\{\Delta y_R \cdot \Delta x_I\} & E\{\Delta y_R \cdot \Delta y_I\} & E\{\Delta y_R \cdot \Delta z_I\} \\ E\{\Delta z_R \cdot \Delta x_I\} & E\{\Delta z_R \cdot \Delta y_I\} & E\{\Delta z_R \cdot \Delta z_I\} \end{bmatrix} = C^T_{IR} \tag{27}$$

(For the statistical relations of the various terms see [1] and Appendix B).

In our case, we have 3 degrees of freedom in the χ^2 test, so for a choice of the value of γ we use a value from Table 4.1.

So, for example, if we want to pass the test with a probability greater than 99.5% we have to select a threshold value of γ greater than 12.8.

If the condition (24) is satisfied, the above tests of step *1 to 3* are repeated, now with the predicted values.

Finally, the mixed detections Ω obtained through the tests 1 to 4 feed the fusion equation. We have all the elements for implementing the fusion equation:

$$\hat{x}(\Omega) = \alpha \cdot \hat{\xi}_R + (1-\alpha) \cdot \hat{\xi}_I \tag{28}$$

The covariance matrix R of the error on $\hat{x}(\Omega)$ is

$$R = \alpha^2 \cdot P_R + (1-\alpha)^2 \cdot P_I + \alpha \cdot (1-\alpha) \cdot (C_{RI} + C_{IR}) \tag{29}$$

where α is given by (17).

Table 4.1. χ^2 table for a χ^2 random variable with 3 degrees of freedom

Probability	0.9	0.95	0.975	0.99	0.995	0.999	0.9995	0.9999
γ		6.25	7.81	9.35	11.3	12.8	16.3	17.7	21.1

5. THE JPDA ALGORITHM AND THE TRACKS TO TRACKS ASSOCIATION ISSUE

A possible solution to the problem of wrong association, after the test (22) and (24), is the use of the Joint Probabilistic Data Association (JPDA) algorithm (see Chapter 6 of [4] and Chapter 6 of [5]), with some adaptations.

When two objects are seen on a small angle, even if they could be at greatly differing distances they will have two close tracks in the *angular space*. In that condition, test (22) could pass regardless of the ranges since the test is required to consider the angular data only (the *common data*). Moreover, if these objects are moving with equal speed it could happen that even test (24) of Step 3 can pass thus causing wrong association of RADAR and IRST tracks having up to 4 mixed detections instead of the expected 2.

Now let us designate

$$c = \left(\hat{\xi}_R - \hat{\xi}_I \right)^T \cdot P^{-1} \cdot \left(\hat{\xi}_R - \hat{\xi}_I \right) \tag{30}$$

the result of the χ^2 test (24) and c_1 and c_2 specifically the values by which the same RADAR track passes the association test with both IRST tracks. The values c_1 and c_2 are χ^2 distributed. If

$$|c_1 - c_2| > C \tag{31}$$

C being suitably selected, the mixed detection with higher value of c can be rejected.

In all the other cases, i.e., when $|c_1 - c_2| < C$, we will use the classical JPDA algorithm with the following adaptations: the RADAR tracks and the IRST tracks are managed as tracks and detections, respectively, in the generation of the *Validation and Events Matrices* of the classical JPDA algorithm.

Before proceeding further, we must take a short digression in order to provide a brief introduction to the Joint Probabilistic Data Association algorithm and its terminology.

5.1. JPDA in Brief

We will introduce the Joint Probabilistic Data Association algorithm following Yaakov Bar-Shalom, Chapter 6 of [5], where it is provided a more complete and detailed treatment of the subject. The treatment is made for a single sensor case and the hypothesis at the basis of JPDA is: *each target can originate one detection only.*

Let us designate as $Z(k) = \{z_q(k)\}_{q=1}^{N_D}$ the set of N_D detections (measurements) at time k. Now because of the common detections the events arising from such a situation must be considered jointly. For better understanding let us consider the case of Figure 4, where the gates of the tracks related to the two targets T_1 and T_2 share the detection z_2, while z_1 lies in the gate of T_1 and z_3 in the one of T_2.

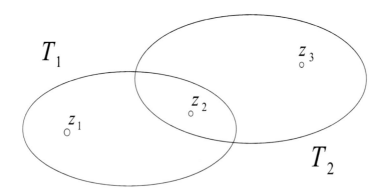

Figure 4.

The situation of Figure 4 can be represented by a matrix, the Validation Matrix Θ, whose elements are:

$$\omega_{rt} = \begin{cases} 1 & \textit{if } z_r \textit{ is considered true and lies in the gate of the track } T_t \\ 0 & \textit{otherwise} \end{cases}$$

For the case of Figure 4 it is

$$\Theta = \begin{bmatrix} 1 & 0 \\ 1 & 1 \\ 0 & 1 \end{bmatrix}$$

From Θ it is immediately evident that z_2 is common to both tracks, while z_1 and z_3 lie, respectively, in the gate of T_1 and T_2 as per Figure 4. So starting from the basic hypothesis, from the Validation Matrix Θ, we can have the following joint events (disregarding those events involving detections which do not belong to a given track gate whose probability is virtually zero):

$$\vartheta_0 = \{ z_1, z_2 \textit{ and } z_3 \textit{ are false} \}$$
$$\vartheta_1 = \{ z_1 \in T_1, z_2 \textit{ and } z_3 \textit{ are false} \}$$
$$\vartheta_2 = \{ z_2 \in T_1, z_1 \textit{ and } z_3 \textit{ are false} \}$$
$$\vartheta_3 = \{ z_2 \in T_2, z_1 \textit{ and } z_3 \textit{ are false} \}$$
$$\vartheta_4 = \{ z_3 \in T_2, z_1 \textit{ and } z_2 \textit{ are false} \}$$
$$\vartheta_5 = \{ z_1 \in T_1, z_2 \in T_2, z_3 \textit{ is false} \}$$
$$\vartheta_6 = \{ z_1 \in T_1, z_3 \in T_2, z_2 \textit{ is false} \}$$
$$\vartheta_7 = \{ z_2 \in T_1, z_3 \in T_2, z_1 \textit{ is false} \}$$

Each of the feasible events ϑ_q can be represented by a suitable matrix Θ_q, the Event Matrix, similar to the Validation one, by defining each of its elements ϑ_{rt} as:

$$\vartheta_{rt} = \begin{cases} 1 & \textit{if } z_r \in T_t \textit{ in the event } \vartheta_q \\ 0 & \textit{otherwise} \end{cases}$$

Moreover a further column is added "*0*," "*no detection to track association*," whose elements are:

$$\vartheta_{r0} = \begin{cases} 1 & \textit{if } z_r \textit{ does not belong to any track in the event } \vartheta_q \\ 0 & \textit{otherwise} \end{cases}.$$

So the sum of the elements of column "*0*" provides the number of false alarms and/or an indicator of no detection association in the event under analysis. For example, the event ϑ_5 is represented by the Event Matrix:

$$\Theta_5 = \begin{bmatrix} 0 & 1 & 0 \\ 0 & 0 & 1 \\ 1 & 0 & 0 \end{bmatrix}.$$

Through Θ_5, it is possible to notice that the detections z_1 and z_2 are deemed true and associated to the tracks T_1 and T_2, respectively, while z_3 is considered a false alarm.

For each column t of Θ_q, a variable d_t is defined, the *detection target indicator*, as:

$$d_t = \sum_{r=1}^{N_D} \vartheta_{rt} \qquad t = 1, 2, \cdots, N_T$$

being N_T the number of tracks in the Validation Matrix. Notice that in the summation the column "*0*" of "*no detection to track association or false associations*" is excluded. The term d_t is called *detection target indicator* because it indicates whether a target is detected through the association with a given measurement. So for every Event Matrix Θ_q, there is a vector, $\delta_q = [d_1 \cdots d_{N_T}]$, made from the detection indicators of each target.

In the same way, for each row r of the Event Matrix Θ_q the *measurement association indicator* is defined as:

$$m_r = \sum_{t=1}^{N_T} \vartheta_{rt} \qquad r = 1, 2, \cdots, N_D.$$

Observe that, as before, in the calculation of m_r, the elements of the column "0" are disregarded.

Given the basic hypothesis of JPDA (each detection comes from only one target) it will always be $0 \le d_t \le 1$ and $0 \le m_r \le 1$.

Following [5] the *joint association event probability* for the generic feasible event ϑ_q is given by:

$$P\{\vartheta_q | Z_k\} = \frac{P\{Z(k) | \vartheta_q, N_D, Z_{k-1}\} \cdot P\{\vartheta_q | N_D\}}{\sum\limits_{r=0}^{N_E} P\{Z(k) | \vartheta_r, N_I, Z_{k-1}\} \cdot P\{\vartheta_r | N_I\}}$$

where N_E is the number of all the feasible events, $Z_k = \{Z(q)\}_{q=1}^k$ is the sequence of detections in the time, $P\{Z(k) | \vartheta_q, N_D, Z_{k-1}\}$ is the *likelihood function of the measurements* and $P\{\vartheta_q | N_D\}$ is the *prior probability* of the joint association event. In particular, considering independent all the detections, the *likelihood function* is given by:

$$P\{Z(k) | \vartheta_q, N_D, Z_{k-1}\} = P\{z_1, z_2, \cdots z_N | \vartheta_q, N_D, Z_{k-1}\} = \prod_{r=1}^{N_D} P\{z_r\}$$

where

$$P\{z_r\} = \begin{cases} G_t(z_r) & \text{if } z_r \text{ is true and belongs to } T_t \text{ in the event } \vartheta_q \\ \dfrac{1}{V} & \text{otherwise} \end{cases}$$

with

$$G_t(z_r) = \frac{e^{-\frac{[z_r - \hat{z}_t(k|k-1)]^T \cdot S^{-1} \cdot [z_r - \hat{z}_t(k|k-1)]}{2}}}{\sqrt{(2 \cdot \pi)^3 \cdot |S|}}$$

the Gaussian *pdf* of the track T_t, being $\hat{z}_t(k|k-1)$ the prediction made for the track T_t at the previous scan for the current one, S the covariance matrix of the residue $z - \hat{z}_t(k|k-1)$ and V the volume of the surveillance region. The term $\dfrac{1}{V}$ in the expression of $P\{z_r\}$ assumes that the *not associated measurements* are considered uniformly distributed in the entire surveillance region.

From [5] the *prior probability* of the joint association event is

$$P\{\vartheta_q | N_D\} = p_{fa}(N_\phi) \cdot \frac{N_\phi!}{N_D!} \prod_{t=1}^{N_T} P_{Dt}^{\delta_q[t]} \cdot (1 - P_{Dn})^{1 - \delta_q[t]}$$

with P_{Dt} the detection probability, in general considered constant for the sensor of interest, N_ϕ the number of false alarms and $p_{fa}(N_\phi)$ false alarm probability in the event ϑ_q.

Due to the use of JPDA in a data fusion context, we must redefine the *detection* and *false alarm probability* as well we have to introduce the *probability of false* and *missed association*. Moreover we have to underline that, due to the rules of track-to-track association, the multiple tracks association can occur for the proximity of some tracks in the field of view of one of the sensors and not only in the presence of crossing tracks, as in the case of single sensor multiple tracking.

Let now N_I be the number of IRST tracks shared by (associated to) multiple RADAR tracks in the Validation Matrix and Θ_q the Event

Matrix related to the event ϑ_q of one of the N_E feasible events. Designate now $Z(k) = \{z_q(k)\}_{q=1}^{N_I}$ as the set of IRST tracks at time k and $Z_k = \{Z(q)\}_{q=1}^{k}$ as the sequence of IRST tracks up to the time k. Following [5] the canonical equation for the feasible event ϑ_q in the modified JPDA algorithm is:

$$P\{\vartheta_q | Z_k\} = \frac{P\{Z(k) | \vartheta_q, N_I, Z_{k-1}\} \cdot P\{\vartheta_q | N_I\}}{\sum_{r=0}^{N_E} P\{Z(k) | \vartheta_r, N_I, Z_{k-1}\} \cdot P\{\vartheta_r | N_I\}} \tag{32}$$

where, for the independence of the IRST tracks, it is

$$P\{Z(k) | \vartheta_q, N_I, Z_{k-1}\} = P\{z_1, z_2, \cdots z_N | \vartheta_q, N_I, Z_{k-1}\} = \prod_{r=1}^{N_I} P\{z_r\} \tag{33}$$

with:

$$P\{z_r\} = \begin{cases} G_m(z_r) & \text{if } z_r \text{ is true in the event } \vartheta_q \\ P_{fa}(z_r) & \text{otherwise} \end{cases} \tag{34}$$

and

$$G_m(z_r) = \frac{e^{-\frac{c}{2}}}{\sqrt{(2 \cdot \pi)^3 \cdot |P|}} \tag{35}$$

Equation (35), with c given by (30), is the Gaussian *pdf* of the mixed detection m made up by IRST track i and RADAR track t, while P_{fa} the *false association probability* between the RADAR and IRST tracks involved in the mixed detection (observe that each element of Θ_q matrix is now related to one mixed detection). The last term in the numerator of (32) is now modified in:

$$P\{\vartheta_q|N_I\}= p_{ft}(N_\phi)\cdot \frac{N_\phi!}{N_I!}\prod_{r=1}^{N_R} P_{Dr}^{\delta_q[r]}\cdot P_{md\ r}^{1-\delta_q[r]} \tag{36}$$

where now $p_{ft}(N_\phi)$ is the *false alarm probability*, P_{Dr} the *detection probability* of RADAR track T_r, $P_{md\ r}$ the *probability of missed association* of T_r and finally $\delta_q[r]$ the target detection indicator of T_r in the Θ_q matrix.

In the single sensor JPDA algorithm described above, equation (36) would use the expression $(1-P_{Dr})^{\delta_q[r]}$ in place of $P_{md\ r}^{1-\delta_q[r]}$. However, as we will see later, in contrary to the single sensor case where a not detected track is determined by the lack of detection inside the track gate, in the data fusion context the missed detection of a RADAR track has to be considered jointly. That because the missed detection of a RADAR is caused by the fact that, in the event ϑ_q, it is not possible to associate the track of interest to any IRST track. N_ϕ in (36) is the number of false associations in the event represented by Θ_q matrix. In the data fusion context each element of an event matrix is still binary valued:

$$\vartheta_{ir} = \begin{cases} 1 & \textit{if the association between IRST track } T_i \textit{ and RADAR track } T_r \textit{ is considered true} \\ 0 & \textit{otherwise} \end{cases}$$

while for the first column (no tracks association column) it is

$$\vartheta_{i0} = \begin{cases} 0 & \textit{if there is at least one association between an IRST track and all the RADAR tracks} \\ 1 & \textit{otherwise} \end{cases}$$

5.2. The Detection Probability

We define *detection probability* as the probability of track-to-track association, given that the tracks from different sensors are really linked to the same object. In our case, it is given by the probability that test (22) of Step 1 and the χ^2 test (24) of the Step 3 pass when both RADAR and IRST tracks are related to the same target. So, if an object is detected by both the sensors, indicated with T_R and T_I the RADAR and IRST tracks, designated by $P_{DR} = P\{D_R|T_R = T_I\}$ and $P_{DI} = P\{D_I|T_R = T_I\}$ the detection probability of RADAR and IRST, respectively, assuming detection processes independent to one another, it shall be

$$P_D(T_R, T_I) = P\{c < \gamma|D_R, D_I, A, T_R = T_I\} \cdot P\{D_R|T_R = T_I\} \cdot P\{D_I|T_R = T_I\} \cdot P\{A|T_R = T_I\}$$

and so

$$P_D(T_R, T_I) = P_{DR} \cdot P_{DI} \cdot P\{c < \gamma|D_R, D_I, A, T_R = T_I\} \cdot P\{A|T_R = T_I\} \qquad (37)$$

with c given by (30) and

$A = \{Test\ (22)\ of\ Step\ 1\ passed\}$.

With being the two tracks of interest related to the same object, we attribute to them a Gaussian distribution with zero mean value. Consequently the difference $\Delta\xi_{RI} = \hat{\xi}_R - \hat{\xi}_I$ in test (24) will be Gaussian distributed with zero mean value too, while c will have probability

$$P_\gamma = P\{c < \gamma|A, T_R = T_I\}$$

and χ^2 pdf. P_γ, obtained through χ^2 table, will just depend on the number of degrees of freedom (3 in this case) and on the selected threshold value γ.

Now, let $\Delta\varphi(k) = \hat{\varphi}(k|k) - \hat{\beta}(k|k)$ and $\Delta\vartheta(k) = \hat{\vartheta}(k|k) - \hat{\eta}(k|k)$ be the azimuth and elevation angular differences, respectively, between the RADAR and IRST data, we have to calculate the probability:

$$P_A = P\{A|T_R = T_I\} = P\{|\Delta\varphi| < K_A \cdot \varepsilon_A, |\Delta\vartheta| < K_E \cdot \varepsilon_E | T_R = T_I\} = P\{A_\varphi, A_\vartheta | T_R = T_I\}$$

(38)

with

$$\begin{cases} A_\varphi = \{|\Delta\varphi| < K_A \cdot \varepsilon_A\} \\ A_\vartheta = \{|\Delta\vartheta| < K_E \cdot \varepsilon_E\} \end{cases}$$

(39)

Since, by hypothesis, the azimuth and elevation angles of both RADAR and IRST are independent:

$$P_A = P\{A_\varphi | T_R = T_I\} \cdot P\{A_\vartheta | T_R = T_I\}$$

So (see Appendix C):

$$P_A = erf\left[\frac{K_A \cdot (\sigma_\varphi + \sigma_\beta)}{\sqrt{2 \cdot (\sigma_\varphi^2 + \sigma_\beta^2)}}\right] \cdot erf\left[\frac{K_E \cdot (\sigma_\vartheta + \sigma_\eta)}{\sqrt{2 \cdot (\sigma_\vartheta^2 + \sigma_\eta^2)}}\right]$$

(40)

By substituting (40) in (37) we obtain:

$$P_D(T_R, T_I) = P_{DR} \cdot P_{DI} \cdot P_\gamma \cdot erf\left[\frac{K_A \cdot (\sigma_\varphi + \sigma_\beta)}{\sqrt{2 \cdot (\sigma_\varphi^2 + \sigma_\beta^2)}}\right] \cdot erf\left[\frac{K_E \cdot (\sigma_\vartheta + \sigma_\eta)}{\sqrt{2 \cdot (\sigma_\vartheta^2 + \sigma_\eta^2)}}\right]$$

(41)

i.e., the *detection probability* as per the above definition. Using (41) we can notice that P_D depends exclusively on the variances of the estimation error of the specific tracks of two sensors which are involved in the generation of mixed detection. This implies that P_D is not a parameter to apply to all the operations of track-to-track association, as in the single sensor case, but rather it is specifically related to each pair of tracks from different sensors.

5.3. Probability of False Association

The *false association probability* $P_{FA}(T_R, T_I)$ is the probability of association of the RADAR and IRST tracks T_R and T_I when they are in fact different objects. In our case, it is the probability that two tracks, linked to different objects, pass the test (22) of Step 1 and the χ^2 test (24) of Step 3, that is:

$$P_{FA}(T_R, T_I) = P\{c < \gamma | E_{RI}\} \tag{42}$$

where

E_{RI} = {*Test (22) of Step 1 passed, given that the two tracks T_R and T_I are not related to the same object*}, in formula:

$$E_{RI} = \{A_\varphi, A_\vartheta | T_R \neq T_I\}$$

with A_φ and A_ϑ defined by (39).

In the Event Matrix Θ_q the elements of the first column indicate the IRST tracks that are not associated to any RADAR track. Hence, if the events E_{RI} are mutually exclusive and exhaustive, the false association probability of the track T_I is given by

$$P_{fa}(T_I) = \sum_{q=1}^{N_R} P_{fa}(T_{Rq}, T_I) = \sum_{q=1}^{N_R} P\{c < \gamma | E_{IRq}\} \cdot P\{E_{IRq}\} \quad I = 1, 2, ..., N_I$$

In the event E_{IRq}, the extraneous track in the *mixed detection* is considered with uniform distribution in the whole surveillance region since, in the absence of information, its estimate can be anywhere. On the contrary, the true track, whose estimate depends on the statistics of its error, is Gaussian distributed. Now the probability of E_{IRq} is (see Appendix D):

$$P\{E_{IRq}\} = 2 \cdot K_A \cdot K_E \cdot (\sigma_\varphi + \sigma_\beta) \cdot (\sigma_\vartheta + \sigma_\eta) \cdot \frac{P_{DR} + P_{DI} - 2 \cdot P_{DR} \cdot P_{DI}}{\pi^2} \quad (43)$$

Since $P\{c < \gamma | E_{IRq}\}$ is conditioned by the event E_{IRq}, it is:

$$P\{c < \gamma | E_{IRq}\} = P\{c < \gamma | T_{Rq} \neq T_I\} = P\{c < \gamma | T_{Rq}, \overline{T}_I\} \cdot P\{T_{Rq}, \overline{T}_I\} + P\{c < \gamma | \overline{T}_{Rq}, T_I\} \cdot P\{\overline{T}_{Rq}, T_I\}$$

where with the notation $\overline{T}_x$ means that the given track from sensor X is "false" (i.e., it is not to associate to the same object).

Hence:

$$P\{c < \gamma | E_{IRq}\} = P\{c < \gamma | T_{Rq}, \overline{T}_I\} \cdot P_{DR} \cdot (1 - P_{DI}) + P\{c < \gamma | \overline{T}_{Rq}, T_I\} \cdot P_{DI} \cdot (1 - P_{DR})$$

In Appendix E it is shown that

$$P\{c < \gamma | E_{IRq}\} = (P_{DR} + P_{DI} - 2 \cdot P_{DR} \cdot P_{DI}) \cdot \left[erf\left(\sqrt{\frac{\gamma}{2}}\right) - 2 \cdot \sqrt{\frac{2 \cdot \gamma}{\pi}} \cdot e^{-\frac{\gamma}{2}} \right] \quad (44)$$

Substituting (43) and (44) in (42), we obtain at last the *false association probability* of the tracks T_R and T_I in the data fusion system:

$$P_{FA}(T_R, T_I) = 2 \cdot K_A K_E (\sigma_\varphi + \sigma_\beta)(\sigma_\vartheta + \sigma_\eta) \frac{(P_{DR} + P_{DI} - 2 \cdot P_{DR} \cdot P_{DI})^2}{\pi^2} \left[erf\left(\sqrt{\frac{\gamma}{2}}\right) - 2 \cdot \sqrt{\frac{2 \cdot \gamma}{\pi}} \cdot e^{-\frac{\gamma}{2}} \right] \quad (45)$$

Again by (45), we can notice that P_{FA} depends on the specific tracks from the two sensors involved in the association process.

Step 4 requires the repetition of tests (22) and (24) using the predicted data in the process of association between tracks from different sensors. Designated by $P_D(k|k)$, the estimated detection probabilities, $P_{FA}(k|k)$, the estimated false association probabilities, $P_D(k+1|k)$, the predicted detection probabilities, $P_{FA}(k+1|k)$, the predicted false association probabilities, the final detection and false association probabilities will be

$$\begin{cases} P_{fa} = P_{FA}(k|k) \cdot P_{FA}(k+1|k) \\ P_d = P_D(k|k) \cdot P_D(k+1|k) \end{cases} \tag{46}$$

5.4. Probability of Missed Association

For the evaluation of the *probability* of the event ϑ_q, we need the probabilities of detection P_d and missed association. The former is provided by (46) while the latter will now be calculated.

In the event where there is no detection of the track of interest, the *missed detection probability* P_{md}, obtained considering the target is present in both of the relevant fields of view, has to be evaluated. Then we define the *missed association probability*, P_{MISS}, as the probability of not generating the mixed detection relevant to two RADAR and IRST tracks, given the current (estimated) and predicted tracks. Since a mixed detection is obtained through two steps, the first by using the estimated data and the second, using the predicted data, by designating $P_{MISS}(k|k)$ and $P_{MISS}(k+1|k)$ the aforementioned probabilities, we have:

$$P_{md} = P_{MISS}(k|k) + P_{MISS}(k+1|k) \cdot P_D(k|k) \tag{47}$$

with $P_D(k|k)$ the detection probability (41) for the estimated data. Equation (47) means that a missed detection can occur either when steps 1 and 3 do not pass with the estimation data or when, although those tests pass, they do not for the predicted data. Let us start with $P_{MISS}(k|k)$ omitting the time dependence for simplicity. So for the missed association probability of the RADAR track T_R with the IRST track T_I:

$$P_{MISS}(T_R,T_I)= P\{c>\gamma|A,D_R,D_I,T_R=T_I\} \cdot P\{A|D_R,D_I,T_R=T_I\} \cdot P\{D_R,D_I|T_R=T_I\}+ \\ + P\{\overline{A}|D_R,D_I,T_R=T_I\} \cdot P\{D_R,D_I|T_R=T_I\}$$

But

$$P\{D_R,D_I|T_R=T_I\}= P_{DR} \cdot P_{DI} \text{ and } P\{A|T_R=T_I\}=P_\varphi \cdot P_\vartheta$$

with P_φ and P_ϑ given in Appendix C, while

$$P\{c>\gamma|A,D_R,D_I,T_R=T_I\}=1-P_\gamma.$$

So:

$$P_{MISS}(T_R,T_I)= P_{DR} \cdot P_{DI} \cdot \left[P_\varphi \cdot P_\vartheta \cdot (1-P_\gamma)+ P\{\overline{A}|D_R,D_I,T_R=T_I\} \right] (48)$$

The event $\overline{A}$ is the union of the two mutually exclusive and exhaustive events $\{A_\varphi, \overline{A_\vartheta}\}$ and $\{A_\varphi, A_\vartheta\}-\{A_\varphi, \overline{A_\vartheta}\}$, so, omitting for simplicity the conditioning:

$$P\{\overline{A}\}= P\{A_\varphi, \overline{A_\vartheta}\}+ P\{\overline{A_\varphi}, A_\vartheta\}- P\{\overline{A_\varphi}, \overline{A_\vartheta}\}.$$

Since the events A_φ and A_ϑ are independent, it is:

$$P\left\{A_\varphi, \overline{A_\vartheta}\right\} = P_\varphi \cdot \left(1 - P_\vartheta\right)$$ (49)

$$P\left\{\overline{A_\varphi}, A_\vartheta\right\} = P_\vartheta \cdot \left(1 - P_\varphi\right)$$ (50)

$$P\left\{\overline{A_\varphi}, \overline{A_\vartheta}\right\} = \left(1 - P_\varphi\right) \cdot \left(1 - P_\vartheta\right)$$ (51)

By using (49), (50) and (51) we have:

$$P\left\{\overline{A} | D_R, D_I, T_R = T_I\right\} = 2 \cdot \left(P_\varphi + P_\vartheta\right) - \left(1 + 3 \cdot P_\varphi \cdot P_\vartheta\right)$$ (52)

and substituting (52) in (48) we finally get:

$$P_{MISS}\left(T_R, T_I\right) = P_{DR} \cdot P_{DI} \cdot \left[2 \cdot \left(P_\varphi + P_\vartheta - P_\varphi \cdot P_\vartheta\right) - 1 - P_\varphi \cdot P_\vartheta \cdot P_\gamma\right]$$ (53)

Now the dependency of $P_{MISS}\left(T_R, T_I\right)$ is represented by the terms P_φ and P_ϑ. Equation (53) provides the probability of missed association between the RADAR track T_R and the IRST track T_I, while the first of (46) gives the probability of false association. So, considering the probability of missed association of T_R with different IRST tracks independent:

$$P_{md}\left(T_R\right) = \prod_{q=1}^{N_R} P_{md}\left(T_R, T_{Iq}\right)^{1-m_q} \quad R = 1,2,...,N_R$$ (54)

with $P_{md}\left(T_R, T_{Iq}\right)$ the probability of missed association between the RADAR track T_R and IRST track T_{Iq} given by (53) and m_q the *measurement association indicator* previously described. Notice that in (54), in place of the exponent $1 - m_q$ we could equivalently use, as the exponent, the corresponding element ϑ_{q0} of the column "0" of Θ_q, no track-to-track association column.

5.5. The Probability of False Alarm

The *false alarm probability* $p_{ft}(N_\phi)$ is defined as the probability that at least one of the tracks, involved in the generation of a mixed detection, is false. There are two ways to proceed:

- Considering the false alarm probability depending on the number of false tracks N_ϕ in the Event Matrix Θ_q
- Considering the false alarm probability constant (*diffuse pdf*).

Here we focus on the second case and we set

$$p_{ft}\left(N_\phi\right)= p \qquad\qquad \forall N_\phi$$

where p is a constant of the same magnitude of the product of the *probability of false track* of each sensor. This also because the knowledge of the *false tracks* does not contribute to the knowledge of true tracks. This assumption is in accordance on the *Bayes' postulate* (see 1.4.11 and 2.3.4 of [6]) that, in absence of a prior knowledge, a uniform priority *pdf* should be chosen (note that $p \to 0$ over a very wide observation volume V because $p \propto \dfrac{1}{V}$). When $p \to 0$ it is called *diffuse probability* and is often used as a *prior guess* in the absence of information about the event. The term p_{ft}, that appears in the numerator and denominator in (32), will cancel (when developing the formula, the same probability will appear for event ϑ_q as well for all events ϑ_r), simplifying the calculation of

$P\{\vartheta_q | Z_k\}$. This simplification is valid if the probability of false track of any single sensor system is very small, as is generally true.

5.6. Conclusion

We have just defined all the parameters necessary to run JPDA. Now we use the ability of JPDA to indicate the most probable association to decide whether a mixed detection belongs to a fused track rather than to another. In that way we avoid the well-known coalescence problem related with the JPDA algorithm (Chapter 1 of [7]) i.e the undesired event that a detection shared by multiple tracks tends to stay in a midway position between them and can also cause the loss of one or more of them.

6. RESULTS OF SIMULATIONS

In the upcoming simulations, the RADAR scanning period is set to T_{SR} = *1 sec*, while the IRST one to T_{SI} = *0.157 sec*. The synchronization of data between the two systems is performed by interpolation between samples [1] and we consider the probability of false alarm in the JPDA algorithm to be constant.

We assume that RADAR performs measurements of range with rms error of *75 m*, while the angle has an rms error of *0.5 degrees*. The IRST angular measurement error is *0.6 mrad* rms. The Interacting Multiple Mode (IMM) algorithm (Chapter 4 of [5]) is used for both Track Formation and Established Tracks processes for both the sensors and for the fusion system.

The data fusion system makes use of the fusion equation (16).

Simple but effective scenarios have been characterized. We considered the following figures of merit:

1. The probability of correct association between tracks, i.e., the probability that two tracks from different sensors, fused together, concern the same object [10];
2. The increased precision of the fused tracks with respect to a single-sensor tracking;
3. The absence of bias in the estimation errors along the three coordinates axes.

The first figure of merit, i.e., the probability of correct association between tracks, is evaluated using *2* objects moving along helical paths at very small angular distances and relative speeds as shown in Figure 6. Figure 7 is the graph of the behavior of Correct Associations to Life Time ratio of the Fused Track that approximates the probability of Correct Association of the System of Fusion throughout the tracking period. For analysis of the behaviors of the process in this simulation, we can divide this scenario into three parts:

The first part, lasting approximately 100 seconds, sees the two objects at angular distances less than 1 degree while the first 100 samples of the graph in Figure 7 represent the behavior of the Correct Associations to Life time ratio. Because of the error of angular estimate of both sensors, the test of association (22) of Step 1 can pass even with a distance greater than 1 degree between tracks. Furthermore, since the motions of the two objects are very similar, also test (24) of Step 3 has a high probability to pass with the generation of 3 to 4 mixed detections instead of 2. In this phase of the test, it can happen that some mixed detections are discarded because of the test (31). The algorithm JPDA is still active in this part of the scenario leading to a probability of correct association always close to 100%, as it is shown by the graph of Figure 7.

In the second part of the scenario the gates of both the sensors tracks merge with each other and they tend to coincide. In such circumstances, the almost identical states of motion of the two targets and the presence of measurement noise make the "histories" of the involved targets ineffective in determining what mixed detection belong to one or the other fused track. Furthermore it must be noted that JPDA algorithms used by RADAR and

IRST can fail in performing the correct detection-track associations without any additional information. In such a case, the states of the almost identical motion of the two targets and the presence of measurement noise determine a continuous switching between correct and false association, as is evident in the part of the graph of Figure 7 from the samples 100 to 220. Let us observe, however, that fused tracks obtained from these wrong associations still continue to be consistent and stable until the motions of the tracks are almost equal.

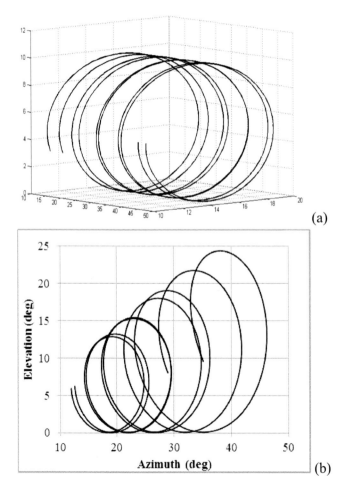

(a)

(b)

Figure 6. (a) Objects in RADAR coordinates (X Y axes only); (b) Objects in IRST coordinates.

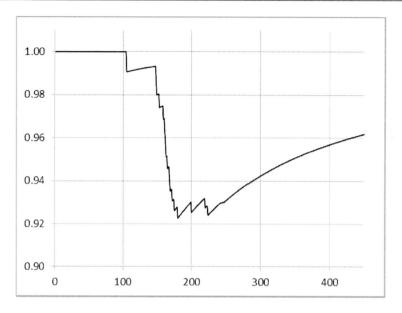

Figure 7. Correct Associations/Lifetime Ratio.

In the third part, the tracks begin to separate. Now the JPDA algorithm is able to distinguish between the mixed detections without ambiguity so that the probability of correct association returns to increment tending virtually to 100% (part 220 to 450 of the curve of Figure 7).

The second figure of merit, i.e., the increased precision of the fused tracks with respect to a single-sensor tracking, is evaluated against an object placed at a distance of about *70 Km* which approaches the observer at constant altitude, at *45 degrees* off axis, and at *250 Km/h* constant speed along X and Y directions. In particular, a number of *50* Monte Carlo runs were carried out during which the estimation errors $\Delta x_q(k)$, $\Delta y_q(k)$ and $\Delta z_q(k)$ were measured. Figure 8 shows the behavior of the total mean estimation error, $\mu_T(k)$, of RADAR and of the fusion system evaluated by means:

$$\mu_T(k) = \frac{1}{N} \cdot \sum_{q=1}^{N} \sqrt{\Delta x_q^2(k) + \Delta y_q^2(k) + \Delta z_q^2(k)} \,..$$

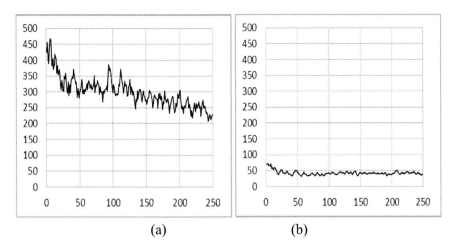

Figure 8. Mean estimation error (m) vs. time: (a) RADAR mean estimation error; (b) Data Fusion mean estimation error (m).

The third figure of merit, i.e., the absence of bias in the estimation errors along the three coordinates axes, is evaluated by computing the normalized mean estimation error (NMEE) (Chapter 5 of [6]) along the three coordinates axes based on previous N Monte Carlo runs:

$$\mu(k) = \frac{1}{N} \cdot \sum_{q=1}^{N} \frac{\Delta x_q(k)}{\sigma_q} \quad , \quad k = 0,1,2,3,\cdots,K \tag{55}$$

σ_q being the standard deviation measured along the K samples in the q-th run of the error component Δx. The term $\xi = \dfrac{\Delta x_q(k)}{\sigma_q}$ appearing in (55) is Gaussian with unity variance and, as we will verify, zero mean valued, i.e., $\mathcal{N}(0,1)$. In this case $\mu(k)$ will also be Gaussian, with zero mean value but with variance $\dfrac{1}{N}$, i.e., $\mathcal{N}(0, 1/N)$. So we can accept the hypothesis that ξ is zero mean valued if there exists a *confidence interval* $[-\psi,\psi]$, where the probability that $\xi \in [-\psi,\psi]$ is equal to $P_\alpha = P\{-\psi \le \xi \le \psi\} = efr(\psi)$.

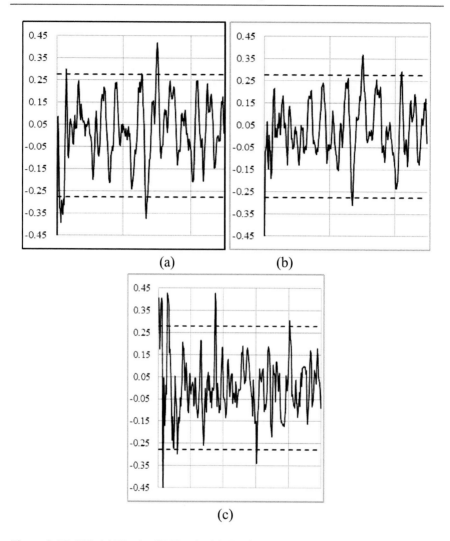

Figure 9. NMEE: (a) X axis; (b) Y axis; (c) Z axis.

Using a two-side confidence interval of 95%, which we have set due to the size of our simulations, by means of the table of the zero-mean unity-variance normal random variable $\mathcal{N}$ $(0,1)$, we achieve $\psi = 1.967$. Since $\mu(k)$ is $\mathcal{N}(0,\ 1/N)$, the confidence interval will be $\left[-\dfrac{1.967}{\sqrt{N}}, \dfrac{1.967}{\sqrt{N}}\right]$. By using $N = 50$, as in our Monte Carlo runs of length $K = 250$ samples, our hypothesis, that the true mean of state estimation error will be zero, is accepted if:

$$\mu(k) \in [-0.2781, 0.2781].$$

Figure 9, (a), (b), (c) show the normalized mean error along the *3* coordinates axes together with the limits of the tolerance interval of *95%*. It is possible to observe that the curves are all within the confidence interval, except for few isolated periods.

CONCLUSION

The subjects of this chapter provide some simple and effective solutions in general and specifically for Radar and IRST data fusion.

Tests have been made in simulation and real environment. The algorithms appear to be fast, consistent and robust.

Although what has been proposed does not complete all the possible conditions, however, the methods offer useful and effective information for new implementations.

APPENDIX A.

VARIANCES OF THE ERRORS OF AZIMUTH, ELEVATION AND RANGE

To calculate the errors Δr and $\Delta \eta$ we will make use of the series expansion stopping at the first term [2]:

$$\begin{cases} \Delta r(x_R, y_R, z_R) \cong \dfrac{\partial r}{\partial x_R} \cdot \Delta x_R + \dfrac{\partial r}{\partial y_R} \cdot \Delta y_R + \dfrac{\partial r}{\partial z_R} \cdot \Delta z_R \\[3mm] \Delta \eta(x_R, y_R, z_R) \cong \dfrac{\partial \eta}{\partial x_R} \cdot \Delta x_R + \dfrac{\partial \eta}{\partial y_R} \cdot \Delta y_R + \dfrac{\partial \eta}{\partial z_R} \cdot \Delta z_R \end{cases} \qquad (A1)$$

whence:

$$\Delta r = \frac{x_R \Delta x_R}{r} + \frac{y_R \Delta y_R}{r} + \frac{z_R \Delta z_R}{r} = (\Delta x_R \cdot \cos \beta + \Delta y_R \cdot \sin \beta) \cdot \cos \eta + \Delta z_R \cdot \sin \eta \quad (A2)$$

and

$$\Delta \eta \cong -\frac{x_R \cdot z_R}{r_{xy} \cdot r^2} \cdot \Delta x_R - \frac{y_R \cdot z_R}{r_{xy} \cdot r^2} \cdot \Delta y_R + \frac{r_{xy}}{r^2} \cdot \Delta z_R \quad (A3)$$

From (A2) and (A3) we can consider Δr and $\Delta \eta$ Gaussian, with zero mean as Δx_R, Δy_R and Δz_R. Proceeding as previously also for $\Delta \beta$ and Δr_{xy} we have:

$$\begin{cases} \Delta \beta \cong -\frac{y_R}{r_{xy}^2} \cdot \Delta x_R + \frac{x_R}{r_{xy}^2} \cdot \Delta y_R \\ \Delta r_{xy} \cong \frac{x_R \Delta x_R}{r_{xy}} + \frac{y_R \Delta y_R}{r_{xy}} = \Delta x_R \cdot \cos \beta + \Delta y_R \cdot \sin \beta \end{cases}$$

so, [1]:

$$\begin{cases} \sigma_\beta^2 = E\{\Delta\beta^2 | \hat{r}_{xy}, \hat{x}_R, \hat{y}_R\} = \frac{\hat{y}_R^2 \cdot \sigma_x^2 + \hat{x}_R^2 \cdot \sigma_y^2 - 2 \cdot \hat{x}_R \cdot \hat{y}_R \cdot \rho_{xy}}{\hat{r}_{xy}^4} + 2 \cdot \frac{\sigma_x^2 \cdot \sigma_y^2 - \rho_{xy}^2}{\hat{r}_{xy}^4} \\ \sigma_{r_{xy}}^2 = E\{\Delta^2 r_{xy} | \hat{r}_{xy}, \hat{x}_R, \hat{y}_R\} = E\{\Delta^2 r_{xy} | \hat{\beta}\} = e^{-\sigma_\beta^2} [\sigma_x^2 \cdot (\cosh \sigma_\beta^2 \cdot \cos^2 \hat{\beta} + \sinh \sigma_\beta^2 \cdot \sin^2 \hat{\beta}) + \\ + \sigma_y^2 \cdot (\cosh \sigma_\beta^2 \cdot \sin^2 \hat{\beta} + \sinh \sigma_\beta^2 \cdot \cos^2 \hat{\beta}) + 2 \cdot \rho_{xy} \sin \hat{\beta} \cdot \cos \hat{\beta}] \end{cases}$$

$$(A4)$$

For the calculation of the variance of the estimation error of the range it will be:

$$E\{\Delta^2 r | x_R, y_R, z_R\} = E\{(\Delta x_R \cdot \cos\beta + \Delta y_R \cdot \sin\beta + \Delta z_R \cdot \sin\eta)^2 | \beta, \eta\}$$

whence:

$$E\{\Delta^2 r | \beta, \eta\} = (\sigma_x^2 \cdot \cos^2\beta + \sigma_y^2 \cdot \sin^2\beta) \cdot \cos^2\eta + \sigma_z^2 \cdot \sin^2\eta$$
$$+ 2 \cdot \rho_{xy} \cdot \cos\beta \cdot \sin\beta \cdot \cos\eta + 2 \cdot (\rho_{xz} \cdot \cos\beta + \rho_{yz} \cdot \sin\beta) \cdot \sin\eta \cdot \cos\eta$$

Since we only have estimates of the quantities:

$$\sigma_r^2 = E\{\Delta^2 r | \hat{\beta}, \hat{\eta}\} = E\{[\sigma_x^2 \cdot \cos^2(\hat{\beta} - \Delta\beta) + \sigma_y^2 \cdot \sin^2(\hat{\beta} - \Delta\beta)] \cdot \cos^2(\hat{\eta} - \Delta\eta) + \sigma_z^2 \cdot \sin^2(\hat{\eta} - \Delta\eta)$$
$$+ 2 \cdot \rho_{xy} \cdot \cos(\hat{\beta} - \Delta\beta) \cdot \sin(\hat{\beta} - \Delta\beta) \cdot \cos(\hat{\eta} - \Delta\eta)$$
$$+ 2 \cdot [\rho_{xz} \cdot \cos(\hat{\beta} - \Delta\beta) + 2 \cdot \rho_{yz} \cdot \sin(\hat{\beta} - \Delta\beta)] \cdot \sin(\hat{\eta} - \Delta\eta) \cdot \cos(\hat{\eta} - \Delta\eta) | \hat{\beta}, \hat{\eta}\}$$

(A5)

from which:

$$\sigma_r^2 = [\sigma_x^2 \cdot (\cosh\sigma_\beta^2 \cdot \cos^2\hat{\beta} + \sinh\sigma_\beta^2 \cdot \sin^2\hat{\beta}) + \sigma_y^2 \cdot (\cosh\sigma_\beta^2 \cdot \sin^2\hat{\beta} + \sinh\sigma_\beta^2 \cdot \cos^2\hat{\beta})]$$
$$\times (\cosh\sigma_\eta^2 \cdot \cos^2\hat{\eta} + \sinh\sigma_\eta^2 \cdot \sin^2\hat{\eta}) \cdot e^{-(\sigma_\beta^2 + \sigma_\eta^2)}$$
$$+ \sigma_z^2 \cdot e^{-\sigma_\eta^2} \cdot (\cosh\sigma_\eta^2 \cdot \sin^2\hat{\eta} + \sinh\sigma_\eta^2 \cdot \cos^2\hat{\eta}) + 2 \cdot \rho_{xy} \cdot e^{-\left(2\cdot\sigma_\beta^2 + \frac{\sigma_\eta^2}{2}\right)} \cdot \sin\hat{\beta} \cdot \cos\hat{\beta} \cdot \cos\hat{\eta}$$
$$+ 2 \cdot (\rho_{xz} \cdot \cos\hat{\beta} + \rho_{yz} \cdot \sin\hat{\beta}) \cdot e^{-\left(\frac{\sigma_\beta^2}{2} + 2\cdot\sigma_\eta^2\right)} \cdot \sin\hat{\eta} \cdot \cos\hat{\eta}$$

(A6)

For the calculation of the variance of η:

$$E\{\Delta^2\eta | x_R, y_R, z_R\} = \frac{x_R^2 \cdot z_R^2}{r_{xy}^2 \cdot r^4} \cdot \sigma_x^2 + \frac{y_R^2 \cdot z_R^2}{r_{xy}^2 \cdot r^4} \cdot \sigma_y^2 + \frac{r_{xy}^2}{r^4} \cdot \sigma_z^2 + 2 \cdot \frac{x_R \cdot y_R \cdot z_R^2}{r_{xy}^2 \cdot r^2} \cdot \rho_{xy}$$
$$- 2 \cdot \frac{x_R \cdot z_R}{r^4} \cdot \rho_{xz} - 2 \cdot \frac{y_R \cdot z_R}{r^4} \cdot \rho_{yz}$$

(A7)

Putting $\sigma_\eta^2 = E\{\Delta^2 \eta | \hat{x}_R, \hat{y}_R, \hat{z}_R\}$, (A7) becomes:

$$\sigma_\eta^2 = E\left\{ \frac{(\hat{x}_R - \Delta x_R)^2 \cdot (\hat{z}_R - \Delta z_R)^2}{\hat{r}_{xy}^2 \cdot \hat{r}^4} \cdot \sigma_x^2 + \frac{(\hat{y}_R - \Delta y_R)^2 \cdot (\hat{z}_R - \Delta z_R)^2}{\hat{r}_{xy}^2 \cdot \hat{r}^4} \cdot \sigma_y^2 + \right.$$
$$+ \frac{(\hat{r}_{xy} - \Delta r_{xy})^2}{r^4} \cdot \sigma_z^2 + 2 \cdot \frac{(\hat{x}_R - \Delta x_R) \cdot (\hat{y}_R - \Delta y_R) \cdot (\hat{z}_R - \Delta z_R)^2}{r_{xy}^2 \cdot r^4} \cdot \rho_{xy} +$$
$$\left. - 2 \cdot \frac{(\hat{x}_R - \Delta x_R) \cdot (\hat{z}_R - \Delta z_R)}{r^4} \cdot \rho_{xz} - 2 \cdot \frac{(\hat{y}_R - \Delta y_R) \cdot (\hat{z}_R - \Delta z_R)}{r^4} \cdot \rho_{yz} \Big| \hat{x}_R, \hat{y}_R, \hat{z}_R \right\}$$

(A8)

Moreover, considering that $E\{\Delta x_R \cdot \Delta y_R \cdot \Delta z_R\} = 0$ and that for two jointly Gaussian random variables ξ and ζ, with zero mean, variances σ_ξ^2, σ_ζ^2, and correlation coefficient ρ:

$$E\{\xi^2 \cdot \zeta^2\} = \sigma_\xi^2 \cdot \sigma_\zeta^2 + 2 \cdot E^2\{\xi \cdot \zeta\}$$

(A9)

and

$$E\{\xi \cdot \zeta^2\} = E\{\xi \cdot E\{\zeta^2 | \xi\}\} = E\{\xi \cdot \sigma_\zeta^2 \cdot (1 - \rho^2)\} = \sigma_\zeta^2 \cdot (1 - \rho^2) \cdot E\{\xi\} = 0$$

(A10)

we have:

$$\sigma_\eta^2 = \frac{\sigma_x^4 + \sigma_y^4 + \hat{x}_R^2 \cdot \sigma_x^2 + \hat{y}_R^2 \cdot \sigma_y^2 + 2 \cdot \rho_{xy} \cdot (\hat{x}_R \cdot \hat{y}_R + \rho_{xy})}{\hat{r}_{xy}^2 \cdot \hat{r}^4} \cdot (\hat{z}_R^2 + \sigma_z^2) +$$
$$+ 2 \cdot \frac{\rho_{xz} \cdot \sigma_x^2 \cdot (\rho_{xz} + 2 \cdot \hat{x}_R \cdot \hat{z}_R) + \rho_{yz} \cdot \sigma_y^2 \cdot (\rho_{yz} + 2 \cdot \hat{y}_R \cdot \hat{z}_R) - 2 \cdot \hat{z}_R \cdot \rho_{xy} \cdot (\hat{x}_R \cdot \rho_{yz} + \hat{y}_R \cdot \rho_{xz})}{\hat{r}_{xy}^2 \cdot \hat{r}^4} +$$
$$+ \frac{(\hat{r}_{xy}^2 + \sigma_{r_{xy}}^2) \cdot \sigma_z^2 - 2 \cdot [\rho_{xz}^2 + \rho_{yz}^2 + \hat{z}_R \cdot (\hat{x}_R \cdot \rho_{xz} + \hat{y}_R \cdot \rho_{yz})]}{\hat{r}^4}$$

(A11)

APPENDIX B. CROSS CORRELATION
BETWEEN $\Delta\xi_I$ AND $\Delta\xi_R$

As the expressions of the coordinates of the tracks from the RADAR when transformed from the spherical to Cartesian axis system have the same form of the expression of $\hat{\xi}_I$, even their estimation error presents the same form with β, η, $\Delta\beta$, and $\Delta\eta$ in place of φ, ϑ, $\Delta\varphi$ and $\Delta\vartheta$. In addition, whereas Δr, $\Delta\varphi$, $\Delta\vartheta$, $\Delta\beta$ and $\Delta\eta$ are uncorrelated and the mean value of the sine function of a random variable with zero mean value is zero, we get [2]:

$$E\{\Delta x_I \Delta x_R | r,\varphi,\vartheta,\beta,\eta\} = E\{r^2 \cdot \cos\varphi \cdot \cos\vartheta \cdot \cos\beta \cdot \cos\eta \cdot (\cos\Delta\varphi \cdot \cos\Delta\vartheta - 1)(\cos\Delta\beta \cdot \cos\Delta\eta - 1) +$$
$$+ \Delta^2 r \cdot \cos\varphi \cdot \cos\vartheta \cdot \cos\beta \cdot \cos\eta \cdot \cos\Delta\varphi \cdot \cos\Delta\vartheta \cdot \cos\Delta\beta \cdot \cos\Delta\eta | r,\varphi,\vartheta,\beta,\eta\}$$

and so:

$$E\{\Delta x_I \Delta x_R | r,\varphi,\vartheta,\beta,\eta\} = \left[r^2 \cdot \left(e^{-\frac{\sigma_\varphi^2 + \sigma_\vartheta^2}{2}} - 1 \right) \cdot \left(e^{-\frac{\sigma_\beta^2 + \sigma_\eta^2}{2}} - 1 \right) + \right.$$
$$\left. + \sigma_r^2 \cdot e^{-\frac{\sigma_\varphi^2 + \sigma_\vartheta^2 + \sigma_\beta^2 + \sigma_\eta^2}{2}} \right] \cdot \cos\varphi \cdot \cos\vartheta \cdot \cos\beta \cdot \cos\eta$$

As the data we have are estimates we will put $E\{\Delta x_I \Delta x_R\} = E\{\Delta x_I \Delta x_R | \hat{r},\hat{\varphi},\hat{\vartheta},\hat{\beta},\hat{\eta}\}$ so:

$$E\{\Delta x_I \Delta x_R\} = E\left\{ \left[(\hat{r} - \Delta r)^2 \cdot \left(e^{-\frac{\sigma_\varphi^2 + \sigma_\vartheta^2}{2}} - 1 \right) \cdot \left(e^{-\frac{\sigma_\beta^2 + \sigma_\eta^2}{2}} - 1 \right) + \sigma_r^2 \cdot e^{-\frac{\sigma_\varphi^2 + \sigma_\vartheta^2 + \sigma_\beta^2 + \sigma_\eta^2}{2}} \right] \times \right.$$
$$\left. \times \cos(\hat{\varphi} - \Delta\varphi) \cdot \cos(\hat{\vartheta} - \Delta\vartheta) \cdot \cos(\hat{\beta} - \Delta\beta) \cdot \cos(\hat{\eta} - \Delta\eta) | \hat{r},\hat{\varphi},\hat{\vartheta},\hat{\beta},\hat{\eta} \right\}$$

hence:

$$E\{\Delta x_I \Delta x_R\} = \left[\left(\hat{r}^2 + \sigma_r^2\right) \cdot \left(e^{-\frac{\sigma_\varphi^2 + \sigma_\vartheta^2}{2}} - 1\right) \cdot \left(e^{-\frac{\sigma_\beta^2 + \sigma_\eta^2}{2}} - 1\right) + \sigma_r^2 \cdot e^{-\frac{\sigma_\varphi^2 + \sigma_\vartheta^2 + \sigma_\beta^2 + \sigma_\eta^2}{2}} \right] \times$$

$$\times e^{-\frac{\sigma_\varphi^2 + \sigma_\vartheta^2 + \sigma_\beta^2 + \sigma_\eta^2}{2}} \cos\hat{\varphi} \cdot \cos\hat{\vartheta} \cdot \cos\hat{\beta} \cdot \cos\hat{\eta}$$

(B1)

Similarly we get:

$$E\{\Delta y_I \Delta y_R\} = \left[\left(\hat{r}^2 + \sigma_r^2\right) \cdot \left(e^{-\frac{\sigma_\varphi^2 + \sigma_\vartheta^2}{2}} - 1\right) \cdot \left(e^{-\frac{\sigma_\beta^2 + \sigma_\eta^2}{2}} - 1\right) + \sigma_r^2 \cdot e^{-\frac{\sigma_\varphi^2 + \sigma_\vartheta^2 + \sigma_\beta^2 + \sigma_\eta^2}{2}} \right] \times$$

$$\times e^{-\frac{\sigma_\varphi^2 + \sigma_\vartheta^2 + \sigma_\beta^2 + \sigma_\eta^2}{2}} \sin\hat{\varphi} \cdot \cos\hat{\vartheta} \cdot \sin\hat{\beta} \cdot \cos\hat{\eta}$$

(B2)

$$E\{\Delta z_I \Delta z_R\} = \left[\left(\hat{r}^2 + \sigma_r^2\right) \cdot \left(e^{-\frac{\sigma_\vartheta^2}{2}} - 1\right) \cdot \left(e^{-\frac{\sigma_\eta^2}{2}} - 1\right) + \sigma_r^2 \cdot e^{-\frac{\sigma_\vartheta^2 + \sigma_\eta^2}{2}} \right] \times e^{-\frac{\sigma_\vartheta^2 + \sigma_\eta^2}{2}} \sin\hat{\vartheta} \cdot \sin\hat{\eta}$$

(B3)

$$E\{\Delta x_I \Delta y_R\} = \left[\left(\hat{r}^2 + \sigma_r^2\right) \cdot \left(e^{-\frac{\sigma_\varphi^2 + \sigma_\vartheta^2}{2}} - 1\right) \cdot \left(e^{-\frac{\sigma_\beta^2 + \sigma_\eta^2}{2}} - 1\right) + \sigma_r^2 \cdot e^{-\frac{\sigma_\varphi^2 + \sigma_\vartheta^2 + \sigma_\beta^2 + \sigma_\eta^2}{2}} \right] \times$$

$$\times e^{-\frac{\sigma_\varphi^2 + \sigma_\vartheta^2 + \sigma_\beta^2 + \sigma_\eta^2}{2}} \cos\hat{\varphi} \cdot \cos\hat{\vartheta} \cdot \sin\hat{\beta} \cdot \cos\hat{\eta}$$

(B4)

$$E\{\Delta x_R \Delta y_I\} = \left[\left(\hat{r}^2 + \sigma_r^2\right) \cdot \left(e^{-\frac{\sigma_\varphi^2 + \sigma_\vartheta^2}{2}} - 1\right) \cdot \left(e^{-\frac{\sigma_\beta^2 + \sigma_\eta^2}{2}} - 1\right) + \sigma_r^2 \cdot e^{-\frac{\sigma_\varphi^2 + \sigma_\vartheta^2 + \sigma_\beta^2 + \sigma_\eta^2}{2}} \right] \times$$

$$\times e^{-\frac{\sigma_\varphi^2 + \sigma_\vartheta^2 + \sigma_\beta^2 + \sigma_\eta^2}{2}} \sin\hat{\varphi} \cdot \cos\hat{\vartheta} \cdot \cos\hat{\beta} \cdot \cos\hat{\eta}$$

(B5)

$$E\{\Delta x_I \Delta z_R\} = \left[\left(\hat{r}^2 + \sigma_r^2 \right) \cdot \left(e^{-\frac{\sigma_\varphi^2 + \sigma_\vartheta^2}{2}} - 1 \right) \cdot \left(e^{-\frac{\sigma_\eta^2}{2}} - 1 \right) + \sigma_r^2 \cdot e^{-\frac{\sigma_\varphi^2 + \sigma_\vartheta^2 + \sigma_\eta^2}{2}} \right] \times$$

$$\times e^{-\frac{\sigma_\varphi^2 + \sigma_\vartheta^2 + \sigma_\eta^2}{2}} \cos \hat{\varphi} \cdot \cos \hat{\vartheta} \cdot \sin \hat{\eta}$$

(B6)

$$E\{\Delta x_R \Delta z_I\} = \left[\left(\hat{r}^2 + \sigma_r^2 \right) \cdot \left(e^{-\frac{\sigma_\varphi^2 + \sigma_\vartheta^2}{2}} - 1 \right) \cdot \left(e^{-\frac{\sigma_\eta^2}{2}} - 1 \right) + \sigma_r^2 \cdot e^{-\frac{\sigma_\varphi^2 + \sigma_\vartheta^2 + \sigma_\eta^2}{2}} \right] \times$$

$$\times e^{-\frac{\sigma_\varphi^2 + \sigma_\vartheta^2 + \sigma_\eta^2}{2}} \sin \hat{\vartheta} \cdot \cos \hat{\beta} \cdot \cos \hat{\eta}$$

(B7)

$$E\{\Delta y_I \Delta z_R\} = \left[\left(\hat{r}^2 + \sigma_r^2 \right) \cdot \left(e^{-\frac{\sigma_\varphi^2 + \sigma_\vartheta^2}{2}} - 1 \right) \cdot \left(e^{-\frac{\sigma_\eta^2}{2}} - 1 \right) + \sigma_r^2 \cdot e^{-\frac{\sigma_\varphi^2 + \sigma_\vartheta^2 + \sigma_\eta^2}{2}} \right] \times$$

$$\times e^{-\frac{\sigma_\varphi^2 + \sigma_\vartheta^2 + \sigma_\eta^2}{2}} \sin \hat{\varphi} \cdot \cos \hat{\vartheta} \cdot \sin \hat{\eta}$$

(B8)

$$E\{\Delta y_R \Delta z_I\} = \left[\left(\hat{r}^2 + \sigma_r^2 \right) \cdot \left(e^{-\frac{\sigma_\varphi^2 + \sigma_\vartheta^2}{2}} - 1 \right) \cdot \left(e^{-\frac{\sigma_\eta^2}{2}} - 1 \right) + \sigma_r^2 \cdot e^{-\frac{\sigma_\varphi^2 + \sigma_\vartheta^2 + \sigma_\eta^2}{2}} \right] \times$$

$$\times e^{-\frac{\sigma_\varphi^2 + \sigma_\vartheta^2 + \sigma_\eta^2}{2}} \sin \hat{\vartheta} \cdot \sin \hat{\beta} \cdot \cos \hat{\eta}$$

(B9)

APPENDIX C. CALCULATION OF P_A

Since in the calculation of the probability $P_A = P\{A_\varphi, A_\vartheta | T_R = T_I\}$, the events $\{A_\varphi | T_R = T_I\}$ and $\{A_\vartheta | T_R = T_I\}$, defined by (39), are independent, we calculate first

$$P\{A_\varphi | T_R = T_I\} = P\{\Delta\varphi < K_A \cdot \varepsilon_A | T_R = T_I\}.$$

As $\Delta\varphi$ is Gaussian with zero mean value and variance $\sigma_A^2 = \sigma_\varphi^2 + \sigma_\beta^2$, it will be:

$$P_\varphi = P\{|\Delta\varphi| < K_A \cdot \varepsilon_A | T_R = T_I\} = \int_{-K_A \cdot \varepsilon_A}^{K_A \cdot \varepsilon_A} \frac{e^{-\frac{\Delta\varphi^2}{2 \cdot \sigma_A^2}}}{\sqrt{2 \cdot \pi \cdot \sigma_A^2}} d(\Delta\varphi) = erf\left(\frac{K_A \cdot \varepsilon_A}{\sqrt{2} \cdot \sigma_A}\right)$$

and substituting ε_A e σ_A :

$$P_\varphi = erf\left(\frac{K_A \cdot (\sigma_\varphi + \sigma_\beta)}{\sqrt{2 \cdot (\sigma_\varphi^2 + \sigma_\beta^2)}}\right) \tag{C1}$$

as usual

$$erf(x) = \frac{1}{\sqrt{\pi}} \cdot \int_0^x e^{-\xi^2} d\xi .$$

In the same way we will get for the elevation:

$$P_\vartheta = erf\left(\frac{K_E \cdot (\sigma_\vartheta + \sigma_\eta)}{\sqrt{2 \cdot (\sigma_\vartheta^2 + \sigma_\eta^2)}}\right) \tag{C2}$$

So:

$$P_A = erf\left(\frac{K_A \cdot (\sigma_\varphi + \sigma_\beta)}{\sqrt{2 \cdot (\sigma_\varphi^2 + \sigma_\beta^2)}}\right) \cdot erf\left(\frac{K_E \cdot (\sigma_\vartheta + \sigma_\eta)}{\sqrt{2 \cdot (\sigma_\vartheta^2 + \sigma_\eta^2)}}\right) \tag{C3}$$

So using (C3) it is:

$$P_D = P_{DR} \cdot P_{DI} \cdot P_\gamma \cdot erf\left(\frac{K_A \cdot (\sigma_\varphi + \sigma_\beta)}{\sqrt{2 \cdot (\sigma_\varphi^2 + \sigma_\beta^2)}}\right) \cdot erf\left(\frac{K_E \cdot (\sigma_\vartheta + \sigma_\eta)}{\sqrt{2 \cdot (\sigma_\vartheta^2 + \sigma_\eta^2)}}\right) \quad (C4)$$

APPENDIX D. CALCULATION OF P_E

The events when $\{T_R$ is *true* and T_I is *extraneous*$\}$, $\{T_R$ is *extraneous* and T_I is *true*$\}$ are designated by $\left\{T_R, \overline{T}_I\right\}$ and $\left\{\overline{T}_R, T_I\right\}$ respectively, we have:

$$P_E = P\{E_{RI}\} = P\left\{A_\varphi, A_\vartheta \middle| T_R \neq T_R\right\} = P\left\{A_\varphi, A_\vartheta \middle| T_R, \overline{T}_I\right\} \cdot P\left\{T_R, \overline{T}_I\right\} + P\left\{A_\varphi, A_\vartheta \middle| \overline{T}_R, T_I\right\} \cdot P\left\{\overline{T}_R, T_I\right\}$$

where:

$E_{RI} = \{Test\ (21)\ of\ Step\ 1\ passed,\ given\ that\ the\ two\ Tracks\ T_R\ and\ T_I$ *are not related to the same object*$\}$.

With P_{DR} and P_{DI} the detection probability of RADAR and IRST respectively:

$$\begin{cases} P\left\{T_R, \overline{T}_I\right\} = P_{DR} \cdot (1 - P_{DI}) \\ P\left\{\overline{T}_R, T_I\right\} = P_{DI} \cdot (1 - P_{DR}) \end{cases} \quad (D1)$$

so:

$$P_E = P\left\{A_\varphi, A_\vartheta \middle| T_R, \overline{T}_I\right\} \cdot P_{DR} \cdot (1 - P_{DI}) + P\left\{A_\varphi, A_\vartheta \middle| \overline{T}_R, T_I\right\} \cdot P_{DI} \cdot (1 - P_{DR}) \quad (D2)$$

Since the angular measurements are statistically independent, we can proceed with the calculation of P_E as previously performed, factoring the event E_{RI}:

$$P_E = P\{A_\varphi, A_\vartheta | T_R \neq T_R\} = P\{A_\varphi | T_R \neq T_R\} \cdot P\{A_\vartheta | T_R \neq T_R\}$$

hence:

$$P_E = P\{A_\varphi | T_R, \overline{T_I}\} \cdot P\{A_\vartheta | T_R, \overline{T_I}\} \cdot P_{DR} \cdot (1 - P_{DI}) + P\{A_\varphi | \overline{T_R}, T_I\} \cdot P\{A_\vartheta | \overline{T_R}, T_I\} \cdot P_{DI} \cdot (1 - P_{DR})$$

$$(D3)$$

Let us start with $P\{A_\varphi | T_R, \overline{T_I}\}$. In the event $\{A_\varphi | T_R, \overline{T_I}\}$ the angular measurement errors of RADAR track T_R are considered Gaussian, while uniformly distributed in the interval $[-\pi, \pi]$ the ones relevant to T_I when false. So:

$$P\{A_\varphi | T_R, \overline{T_I}\} = P\{\Delta\varphi | < K_A \cdot \varepsilon_A | T_R, \overline{T_I}\} = P\{|\hat{\beta} - \hat{\varphi}| < K_A \cdot \varepsilon_A | T_R, \overline{T_I}\} = \int_{-\pi}^{\pi} \frac{1}{2 \cdot \pi} \cdot \int_{\hat{\varphi} - K_A \cdot \varepsilon_A}^{\hat{\varphi} + K_A \cdot \varepsilon_A} \frac{e^{-\frac{\hat{\beta}^2}{2 \cdot \sigma_\beta^2}}}{\sqrt{2 \cdot \pi \cdot \sigma_\beta^2}} d\hat{\beta} d\hat{\varphi}$$

On the other hand it is:

$$\int_{\hat{\varphi} - K_A \cdot \varepsilon_A}^{\hat{\varphi} + K_A \cdot \varepsilon_A} \frac{e^{-\frac{\hat{\beta}^2}{2 \cdot \sigma_\beta^2}}}{\sqrt{2 \cdot \pi \cdot \sigma_\beta^2}} d\hat{\beta} = \frac{1}{2} \cdot \left[erf\left(\frac{\hat{\varphi} + K_A \cdot \varepsilon_A}{\sqrt{2 \cdot \sigma_\beta^2}} \right) - erf\left(\frac{\hat{\varphi} - K_A \cdot \varepsilon_A}{\sqrt{2 \cdot \sigma_\beta^2}} \right) \right]$$

so putting:

$$\lambda = \frac{K_A \cdot \varepsilon_A}{\sqrt{2 \cdot \sigma_\beta^2}}, \quad L = \frac{\pi}{\sqrt{2 \cdot \sigma_\beta^2}} \quad \text{and} \quad \alpha = \frac{\hat{\varphi}}{\sqrt{2 \cdot \sigma_\beta^2}} \qquad (D4)$$

we have:

$$\int_{-\pi}^{\pi} \frac{1}{2\cdot\pi} \cdot \int_{\hat{\varphi}-K_A\cdot\varepsilon_A}^{\hat{\varphi}+K_A\cdot\varepsilon_A} \frac{e^{-\frac{\hat{\beta}^2}{2\cdot\sigma_\beta^2}}}{\sqrt{2\cdot\pi\cdot\sigma_\beta^2}} d\hat{\beta}d\hat{\varphi} = \int_{-L}^{L} \frac{1}{4\cdot L} \cdot [erf(\alpha+\lambda)-erf(\alpha-\lambda)]d\alpha$$

will give:

$$P\{A_\varphi|T_R,\overline{T}_I\}=\frac{(L+\lambda)\cdot erf(L+\lambda)-(L-\lambda)\cdot erf(L+\lambda)}{2\cdot L} - \frac{e^{-(L+\lambda)^2}-e^{-(L-\lambda)^2}}{2\cdot\sqrt{\pi}\cdot L}$$

(D5)

Equation (D5) can be simplified considering that $L \gg \lambda$ and $L \gg 4$, so $erf(L+\lambda) \cong erf(L-\lambda)=1$ and $e^{-(L+\lambda)^2} \approx e^{-(L-\lambda)^2} = 0$.
Hence:

$$P\{A_\varphi|T_R,\overline{T}_I\}=\frac{K_A\cdot\varepsilon_A}{\pi}=\frac{K_A\cdot(\sigma_\varphi+\sigma_\beta)}{\pi}$$

(D6)

For $P\{A_\vartheta|T_R,\overline{T}_I\}$, we have to limit the range of the elevation angles to $\left[-\frac{\pi}{2},\frac{\pi}{2}\right]$ thus obtaining:

$$P\{A_\vartheta|T_R,\overline{T}_I\}=2\cdot\frac{K_E\cdot\varepsilon_E}{\pi}=2\cdot\frac{K_E\cdot(\sigma_\vartheta+\sigma_\phi)}{\pi}$$

(D7)

with (D6) and (D7) in (D3) we have:

$$P_E = 2\cdot K_A\cdot K_E\cdot(\sigma_\varphi+\sigma_\beta)\cdot(\sigma_\vartheta+\sigma_\eta)\cdot\frac{P_{DR}+P_{DI}-2\cdot P_{DR}\cdot P_{DI}}{\pi^2}$$

(D8)

APPENDIX E. CALCULATION OF $P\{c < \gamma | E\}$

It is:

$$P\{c < \gamma | E\} = P\{c < \gamma | T_R, \overline{T}_I\} \cdot P_{DR} \cdot (1 - P_{DI}) + P\{c < \gamma | \overline{T}_R, T_I\} \cdot P_{DI} \cdot (1 - P_{DR})$$
(E1)

We start with the evaluation of $P\{c < \gamma | T_R, \overline{T}_I\}$ where the RADAR track T_R is considered gaussian while T_I false (i.e., it is not valid for the association) and uniformly distributed in all the field of view. In that case, c is χ^2 distributed with 3 degrees of freedom since $\Delta \xi_{RI} = \hat{\xi}_R - \hat{\xi}_I$, given $\hat{\xi}_I$, is gaussian with mean value $\hat{\xi}_I$. So:

$$P\{c < \gamma | T_R, \overline{T}_I\} = \int_0^\gamma f(c | \xi_I) dc = \int_0^\gamma \frac{\sqrt{c} \cdot e^{-\frac{c}{2}}}{\sqrt{2 \cdot \pi}} dc$$

hence:

$$P\{c < \gamma | T_R, \overline{T}_I\} = erf\left(\sqrt{\frac{\gamma}{2}}\right) - 2 \cdot \sqrt{\frac{2 \cdot \gamma}{\pi}} \cdot e^{-\frac{\gamma}{2}}.$$

It is not difficult to verify that $P\{c < \gamma | T_R, \overline{T}_I\} = P\{c < \gamma | \overline{T}_R, T_I\}$ so that substituting in (E1) we finally get:

$$P\{c < \gamma | E\} = (P_{DR} + P_{DI} - 2 \cdot P_{DR} \cdot P_{DI}) \left[erf\left(\sqrt{\frac{\gamma}{2}}\right) - 2 \cdot \sqrt{\frac{2 \cdot \gamma}{\pi}} \cdot e^{-\frac{\gamma}{2}} \right]$$
(E2)

REFERENCES

[1] Quaranta, C., Balzarotti, G. (April 2013). Technique for RADAR and infrared search and track data fusion. *Optical Engineering* 52(4), 046401.

[2] Quaranta, C., Balzarotti G. A technique for sensors fusion with limited number of common measures. [9474-25]. *Proceedings of SPIE DSS 2015, Volume 9474: Signal Processing, Sensor/Information Fusion, and Target Recognition XXIV.*

[3] Quaranta, C., Balzarotti G. (2008). Probabilistic data association applications to data fusion. *SPIE Opt. Eng.* 47, 027007.

[4] Blackman, S., Popoli, R. *Modern Tracking Systems.* Artech House, Norwood, Massachusetts (1999).

[5] Bar-Shalom, Y., Willet, P. K., Xin Tiang. *Tracking and Data Fusion, A Handbook Of Algorithm,* YBS Publishing, Box U-2157, Storrs (2011).

[6] Bar-Shalom, Y., Rong Li, X., Thiagalingam Kirubarajan. *Estimation with Applications to Tracking and Navigation.* John Wiley and Son.

[7] Bar-Shalom, Y. *Multitarget-Multisensor tracking: Applications and Advances.* Vol I, YBS Publishing, Box U-157, Storrs (1996).

[8] Chang, K. C., Saha, R. K., Bar-Shalom, Y. (October 1997). On optimal track-to-track fusion. *IEEE Transactions on aerospace and electronic systems,* vol. 33, no. 4.

[9] Mahler, Ronald P. S. (August 4, 2000). Optimal/robust distributed data fusion: a unified approach. Proc. SPIE 4052, *Signal Processing, Sensor Fusion, and Target Recognition IX*, 128; doi:10.1117/12. 395064.

[10] Svensson, Daniel, Wintenby, Johannes, Svensson, Lennart (July 6-9, 2009). *Performance Evaluation of MHT and GM-CPHD in a Ground Target Tracking Scenario. 12th International Conference on Information Fusion.* Seattle, WA, US.

INDEX